Because I Am
The Joy of *Being* in a Divine Universe

Because I Am

The Joy of *Being* in a Divine Universe

GERALD F. PENCA

Cover design by Gerald F. Penca and Nicholas Walmsley

SECOND EDITION
All rights reserved, including the right of
reproduction in whole or in part in any form.
Copyright © 2013 by Gerald F. Penca
Published by Gerald F. Penca
www.divineuniverse.org
Manufactured in the United States of America
ISBN: 9780989219808
Library of Congress Catalog Card No: 2011909388
0 9 8 7 6 5 4 3 2 1

My nine-year-old grandson drew a graphic of his thumbprint for the book cover. His art contains the truth, clarity and wonder of youth, a budding curiosity to find out who we are. Thank you Nicholas.

And, I thank the rest of my family and friends for their unwavering support as they patiently watched me stumble through this endeavor. Your help made all the difference. This book is dedicated to all of you.

CONTENTS

Preface	ix
Introduction	xi

PART ONE: EXISTENCE OF A DIVINE UNIVERSE

1	Universal Energy	3
2	Prime Mover	6
3	Time	9
4	Paradox of Free Choice	15
5	Natural Rights	22
6	Ethics and Rules	26
7	Human Spirituality	32
8	Consciousness	37
9	Conclusion	43

PART TWO: A DAY IN THE DIVINE UNIVERSE

First Light

10	Awakening	47
11	Birth	49
12	Attitude	51

Natural World

13	Cycles	53
14	Footprints	55
15	Cataclysmic Events	57

Relationships

16	Family	59
17	Children	61
18	Love	63
19	Sex	66
20	Divorce	69

Life's Work
- 21 On the Road — 72
- 22 Vocation — 74
- 23 Dignity of Labor — 78
- 24 Expectation — 80
- 25 Success — 82

Health
- 26 Eating Habits and Food Choices — 84
- 27 Environment/Lifestyle — 90
- 28 Medical Care — 92
- 29 Aging — 95
- 30 Hazards — 97

Spirituality
- 31 Meditation — 99
- 32 Mysticism — 101

Last Light
- 33 One Candle — 104
- 34 Death — 105
- 35 Afterlife — 109
- 36 Peace — 111

About the Author — 112

PREFACE

*B*ecause I Am is about *Being* in a timeless Divine Universe and embracing our connection to all things. It contains a unique physical and transcendent perspective that has changed my life and may very well change yours.

Why should you care about what *I* think?

Because:

- I chose the road less traveled, seeking the truth
- I am the middle-class heartland, centered but aware of the extremes
- I have no institutionally religious agenda; no exclusionary mission
- I write for the benefit of everyone, not for academic approval
- I seek truth through science and logic, not faith
- My study and interest in this concept is lifelong
- My theory of a Divine Universe applies to everyone
- My philosophy is compatible with believers and non-believers
- My message will challenge and energize you
- My philosophy leads to a comforting sense of self
- Developing an awareness of a Divine Universe will free you from fear
- Embracing this concept will empower you to enrich your life experience

Because I Am is a book for everyday people trying to find some inner peace and a sense of meaning in a challenging world.

Thank you for your interest, and welcome!

INTRODUCTION

Would you like to experience a more meaningful life? If so, this book is for you. It contains a very special idea: being connected to, and a part of, a universal matrix of energy, the Divine Universe. It explores living our lives in an eternal moment where past, present, and future are an illusion. It relates the theory of timelessness to apparent free choice and random consequences. It then examines how positive choices based on heightened awareness enable us to enhance the joy of *Being*.

Because I Am is NOT a religious book though it does explore religious influence on present-day morality. It is for people of all beliefs, religious or nonreligious. It discusses historical use of motivation by fear and development of positive alternatives to foster emotional and spiritual growth.

Because I Am is divided into two parts: Part One discusses the theory of a Divine Universe. Italicized paragraphs highlight the practical benefit of related theoretical ideas. Part Two discusses the reality of living in a Divine Universe.

The term, "God," is reluctantly used to identify the Prime Mover, only because of its universal recognition. In order to appreciate and understand the concept of a Divine Universe, this book speaks of God in the broadest context without any gender or specific religious significance.

I hope our journey leaves you with a lighter step and a more understanding heart. And, most of all, I hope it leads to truth, love, and beauty in your life.

Gerald F. Penca

Because I Am

The Joy of *Being* in a Divine Universe

PART ONE
Existence of a Divine Universe

CHAPTER I
Universal Energy

Being

Because I am
I see winter's gilded sun
Rise above white frosted fields
Icy crystals come undone

Because I am
I hear sharpened breath of life
Helplessness of baby's cry
Stirring of a sleepy wife

Because I am
I smell dew-kissed lilac scent
Mindful of spring's joyful way
Having paid long winter's rent

Because I am
I taste golden summer corn
Fruited child of August heat
Thankful for cornucopia's horn

Because I am
I reassure a saddened friend
Having lost a lifelong love
Witness to our destined end

Because I am
I feel kindred spirit flow
Pulsing source of all that is,
Connected, *much more than I know*

Gazing into the night sky, I see light from stars that burned out long ago. Beside me, the walls of my house appear to be solid matter, though I know they're mostly empty space. The earth beneath my feet journeys along at rapid speed though I don't feel any movement. And, for some reason, I don't fall into space. Is this world fascinating or what? Should I have paid more attention in science class? Probably!

How much do we really know about our home, the universe? In spite of huge advances in scientific knowledge, we struggle to grasp its true nature. Whether looking through a macro or micro lens, our discoveries are exceeded, exponentially, by more questions.

On a macro level, our probes reveal countless galaxies as far as we can see. Even in the local cosmic "neighborhood," going to the store takes awhile. We live on a planet in one of the "suburban" arms of the Milky Way, a spiral galaxy. Leaving home and traveling at the speed of light (186,000 miles per second), it would take about 30,000 light years (a light year is the distance that light can tavel in one year) just to reach the center. It would take about 100,000 light years to travel from edge to edge. At that rate of speed, we would have to live 100,000 years just to cross our galaxy.

The most powerful probes into space reveal countless other galaxies in all directions, apparently without limit—nothing but unending "stuff." Searching for a beginning, scientists theorize that the universe evolved from a "big bang" event, a cosmic explosion of immeasurable dimensions. They say it is possible that universal expansion and contraction produced previous "big bang" events, suggesting we may never find a point of origin. To complicate things, some theorize the existence of parallel universes, where we live many lives at once, side by side.

In our macro world, the universe fascinates us with black holes that consume anything near them, and dark energy lurking in supposedly empty space. Energy appears to be everywhere, visible and invisible. That might explain why, as a child, I was convinced there were monsters under the bed, even though my parents could never see them!

On a micro level, proven macro physical laws break down. Our observations uncover a world of contrary activity. Quantum physics reveals that the smallest particles act randomly, changing from solid matter to wave entities and back again, demonstrating that solid mass is nothing but energy.

In our search for the common denominator of all things, facts and logic point to one inescapable conclusion: the basic ingredient of existence is pure, ever-changing energy. This energy is found in all that is, physical matter, and the supposedly "empty" space between that matter. It is the essence of all that exists. Scientists are confident that everything in the universe is made of the same cosmic "dust." If that is true, we are all children of the cosmos, linked biologically to each other, chemically to the Earth, and atomically to the universe. We are individual energy connected to, and a part of, a great, comprehensive, Universal Energy.

Where does our present understanding leave us? It leaves us with a limitless universe, beyond measurement in time or space. It leaves us with a universe of incomprehensible complexity, an enigma of unfathomable mystery. And it leaves us with a universe that is, most probably, an incredible matrix of pure energy. So, what is the nature of Universal Energy? Can it be physical *and* spiritual?

CHAPTER 2
Prime Mover

Belonging

No stained glass or varnished pews
And no cathedral ceilings
Rather, room for diverse views
Of open thoughts and feelings

Sun-soaked days and starry nights
The backdrop of this forum
Endless string on mental kites
No need for stiff decorum

Spinning earth beneath our feet
Trusting Designer's reason
Watch black empty space retreat
To places without season

Universe as God's own face
A masked substantiation
Sense our own connected place
Nevermore, alienation

There are several theories regarding the existence or non-existence of a Prime Mover or God and Its relationship with the universe. Our lives are distinctly influenced by which theory we follow. This book is concerned with the existence of universal energy and the possibility of that universal energy being God.

God as the Universe seems to be a reasonable and deserving idea. Perhaps it would be more acceptable if we were not taught from childhood that God is separate and apart from all things. In a God-Universe or Divine Energy Universe, all things, existent and nonexistent, share in God's Divinity and are spiritually connected. It would follow then that we, being nothing but pure energy, are in unity with God.

Before I continue, I must keep my atheist friends from running for the exits. My universal energy theory can have the same merit for nonbelievers. Though, in this book, I pursue universal energy on a spiritual level, it can just as easily be viewed as a purely physical phenomenon leading to the same operative conclusions. Just substitute the word "energy" for "God."

Nonbelievers may be even more comfortable with a universal energy concept because they may not carry preconceived religious beliefs. So, please stay with us. This works for everyone.

The universe has all of the attributes that we, in human terms, would expect of a Deity: power beyond imagination, unlimited capability or accomplishment, indeterminate size and form, incomprehensible complexity and yet simplicity, limitless connection, no apparent beginning or end, and a uniformity or energy that appears to be the basis of all that is.

It has been argued that the Universe can't be divine because some things within it are evil, and God can't be evil. Such a position is dependent on the premise that good and evil exist. We will evaluate that argument under the topic of ethics.

Others have argued that our failure to understand the universe is a weak basis for calling it God. I accept that notion as reasonable criticism. But, as any sumo wrestler will tell you, size does matter! We're not just talking about understanding plumbing or the way a window fan works. We're talking about trying to comprehend a universe so immense that human thought processes are inadequate. The cosmos that we perceive is but a speck in that universe. It would help if we stopped thinking of Mother Earth as the center of all things, an ancient myopic view. How long can we ignore the elephant in the room? What *is* this vast incomprehensible puzzle if it's not God?

> *In a Divine Universe we are in* Being *with all things, separately, and collectively. Rather than thinking of God as a father figure in the sky, we now understand God to be inseparable from us. We no longer pray to a God "in heaven" but connect to our inner self for spiritual access. In a Divine Universe, we recognize God in all that is, including us. There is great joy in the idea of not being separate from God.*

God as the Universe is difficult to define in human terms. Our understanding, experience, and emotions are far too limited to describe a Divine Entity. So we struggle using human characterizations of gender, morality, fairness, compassion, love, justice, etc. to describe that which is indescribable. The best we can say is that the Divine Universe is just God in *Being*, or God *experiencing* Itself. The question arises whether that experience takes place in some arrangement or structure.

We like to think of the universe as governed by some sort of comprehensive order, perhaps a master plan. In so doing, we hope to define a foreseeable, measureable, dependable world—an understandable world that will allow us to exercise control. A "Divine Plan" would be nothing more than God in *Being*. What we perceive as a plan is a manifestation of *Being*. God experiencing Itself has no beginning, sequence, or end. It just *"is."* Our misconception that a state of *Being* is governed by a timeline, and our need to organize that time into hours, days, and years, interferes with a deeper understanding of *Being*. It is quite possible that historical time does not exist in the larger event of *Being*. So, let's follow Alice down the rabbit hole and examine our understanding of time.

CHAPTER 3
Time

One Moment

Just an old grandfather
Clock in the hall
Pendulum swinging
But, no time at all

Jeweled gears meshing
And spinning about
Ratchet arm ticking
But no time comes out

Minute and hour hands
Waiting for cue
Locked in position
Since they were brand new

Movement in gearbox
But none on gold face
How can we measure,
Make sense of this place

Savor each instant
Our Life Force sustains
Past, present, and future
One moment contains

The old clock is wiser
Than people may know
With only one instant
Of life to bestow

Giving direction
And showing us how
There's no better way
Than to live in the "now"

One everyday understanding of time leaves many of life's transcendental experiences without an explanation. In an effort to understand these mysteries, I invite you to view time in a totally different way. This new perspective will help to better understand the concept of timelessness, mystical experience, the possibility of time travel, how a timeless universe might affect our choices, and how it enhances *Being* in the present moment. In order to do that, we need to consider two different concepts of time: Sequential (relative) Time and Perpetual (absolute) Time. For those of you reading this at your local watering hole, "happy hour" is an embellished cousin!

Sequential Time is time that we are most familiar with. It is the kind of time we associate with our physical world. We use Sequential Time to measure the flow of human events. We often think of it as a horizontal line going from point A to point B. It enables us to create a history of our lives. Because Sequential Time is linear, events are organized in the past, present, and future. Sequential Time is a human invention that arose out of necessity. How else would we keep track of anniversaries? Though we tend to think of Sequential Time as absolute, or etched in stone, it is an astrological measurement of the Earth's movement around the Sun and is relative, varying according to an observer's position and speed. In other words, separate observers in different locations may observe greater or lesser start-to-finish times *for the same event*.

Einstein's theory of relativity proves that Sequential Time is relative, not absolute. His experiments confirmed that the period of time necessary for an event to occur depends on the position and speed of the observer. To test his theory, we've sent rockets into space with extremely accurate clocks. Prior to departure, the clocks were synchronized with earth clocks. Upon return to Earth, the rocket clocks displayed a time slightly less than the earth clocks. This difference occurred because the rocket traveled at a greater speed than the Earth. By greatly increasing speed, the difference in time becomes more pronounced. Here is an extreme example: a spaceship flown by a twin astronaut, one of two twin brothers, leaves Earth for an extended period of time, traveling near the speed of light. Upon returning to Earth, the spaceship brother has become much younger than his earth-bound twin. This example shows that Sequential Time depends on our relative position and how fast we are traveling. It also scientifically confirms, on a physical level, the possibility of time travel whereby our astronaut, depending on his speed, could conceivably reach a future object or point instantaneously, or in a shorter time than would be necessary according to earth clocks.

Thus, our notion of Sequential Time as absolute time is in conflict with proven scientific fact. The point is that our understanding of the concepts of past and future may be faulty.

To examine whether the past or future exists, I would like to explore a totally different perspective of time: a timeless world where we live in an eternal moment, an instant with no past or future, called Perpetual or absolute time.

Set forth below is an explanation of how Perpetual Time is one eternal, timeless moment containing all that is, including "past," "present," and "future."

First, as a necessary premise to the development of this theory, we must assume that all of the universe's happenings (events) have always simultaneously existed. This assumption is justified if we agree that the universe is Divine. A timeless, Universal God would encompass all events in all of time without any need that they happen in sequence. Further assume, for illustration purposes, that each event is positioned on a transparent sphere, which contains every conceivable event. Each event would then be constantly visible and accessible to any other event through the sphere.

Such a sphere would allow anyone positioned at any event to access all that is. The sphere would be timeless (i.e., have no beginning or end). Any past or future would be an illusion. Only the present moment would exist in perpetual, absolute time containing all that is. In Perpetual Time, anything that *has* happened or *will* happen is available now. The difference between Sequential and Perpetual Time can be further illustrated by the following examples:

Applying Sequential Time, we construct a hypothetical building with several floors, and assign a separate happening or event to each floor. Because we must move from floor to floor to observe the events, we see only one event at a time. We see the first event on the ground floor. After walking up the stairs, we see the second event on floor two. At this point, the ground floor event is "past," and the event on floor three is yet to be experienced, or "future." To organize what we have seen, we create a sequence of events in the order in which they were observed. As a result, the time-observation of each event depends on, or is relative to, the time-observation of all other events in the sequence. In this way, we use Sequential Time to account for our everyday activities. It is historical time in that it plots events in the past, present, and future.

Now, let's examine the idea of Perpetual Time using the same hypothetical building except that in this example there are large exterior windows on each floor, allowing us to stand back and view all of the events *simultaneously*. We no longer have a sequence of observations because all events can be viewed at once. Past and future events on the different floors merge into the present experience. That experience shows that there is only now. Anything that ever happened or will happen is available to us now. Thus, we have immediate access to the past or the future, at any present moment. Perpetual Time is spiritual time. Our ability to access Perpetual Time is an aspect of our Divine Energy. Perpetual Time fosters the concept of *Being* whereby we live only in this moment, with an understanding that this moment has infinite access to all things in all of time.

Our concept of time creates a framework for how we view events, especially those that have no physical explanation. Perpetual Time gives us a "timeless" structure within which to examine such events.

History books are replete with mystical human experiences, such as apparitions and transformations. By shear numbers, it is reasonable to expect that some of these mystical experiences are legitimate. Could they be a result of spiritual time travel within Perpetual Time? Do we get a brief glimpse of the "past" when we experience a feeling that we've seen something before, or been somewhere before, even though we've never actually traveled there? Are we tapping into Perpetual Time when dreams draw on events from our "past" or "future," sending us messages that reveal information beyond our present knowledge? Do premonitions of "future" happenings result from spiritual travel in Perpetual Time? In traumatic moments when people see their lives flash before them in great detail, are those visions a product of timeless replay from our spiritual side? I keep an open mind knowing that a Perpetual-Time universe could explain why these phenomena continue to be experienced.

Time travel may be physical as well as spiritual or a combination of both. It is defined as the concept of moving between different event points without experiencing some or all of the intervening travel delay. Our rocketing twin example illustrated that time travel into the future is possible. Unfortunately, time travel into the past is more problematic, barred by our present understanding of physics. Although, under certain conditions, a space trip back in time to a parallel universe or through a "wormhole" abnormality might be consistent with the theory of relativity.

Another interesting theory concerns directing our energy through the grand matrix to a different place/time without bodily traveling there, as in the Star Trek series. It is a sort of atomic transformation whereby persons or things are able to "dematerialize" their matter, beam it to a distant target, and instantly "rematerialize." Would that be limited to the present, or could we possibly reemerge in the past or future? Could the answer be contained in a better understanding of energy as it relates to Perpetual Time? Beam me up, Scotty!

I don't pretend that Perpetual Time is easy to understand. I experience moments when the haze clears and timelessness comes into focus, but then it is gone. I struggle to present a concept that intermittently eludes me in an effort to reveal its mind-opening potential. I believe Perpetual Time is the key to understanding our Divinity and the concept of *Being*. It may very well hold *the* great secret that explains all else. I suspect scientists will never master the universe until they truly understand Perpetual Time. So, as they say Down Under, "no worries"—though you may have difficulty embracing a timeless world, it will not keep you from continuing on this journey.

> *Living with an awareness of Perpetual Time allows us to avoid worrying about yesterday or tomorrow and rather, to focus on the most precious thing we have, the present moment. Living in the "now" enables us to focus on* Being, *and our Divine connection.*

Perpetual Time, with its present access to past and future events, challenges our beliefs about having control over our destiny. It suggests the possibility of a universal master plan or overriding spiritual design. How, if at all, would that affect our freedom to choose?

CHAPTER 4

Paradox of Free Choice

Guidance

Vain, we claim vague guiding force as "choices"
Thinking all things happen by our hand
Conveniently we shun contrary voices

Rushing by, we fail to understand
Sweet destiny of matrix time and places
Each "accident" referred to as unplanned

Destined choices masked in freewill faces
Giving us a false sense of control
That our ego readily embraces

Less-than-random pieces make the whole
Merging in exact coordination
When you see things from God's lofty knoll

Embrace the flow with trusting resignation
Free choice, a mirage of self-determination

Our Divine Universe is an ongoing, interconnected, fabric of ever-changing physical and spiritual energy. It is all that is, ever was, or ever will be, completely contained in a present eternal moment. It lacks nothing and is perfect in every way. This Omniscient (all knowing) Entity is aware and has complete knowledge of Itself leaving *nothing* unknown.

Enter decision-making man, stage left. Throughout our existence, we spend our life making choices. Those choices create events or outcomes. We believe that we have free will to make choices, and by choosing wisely, are able to advantageously control events. This belief is nurtured by our deep-seated survival instinct. Controlling outcomes increases the probability of specie success. Not having control subjects us to the apparent uncertainty of arbitrary consequences, or as some would call it, fate. But, in a Divine Universe where God is all-knowing, free choice is paradoxical. The eternal moment contains all that is, including all of our choices and outcomes, past, present, and future. Does that mean we choose subject to the parameters of a grand design or plan? I suggest that the answer is both yes and no.

No choice is an isolated affair. Each choice is influenced by historical fabric and channeled by an ongoing complexity of forces, both internal and external. Choices are governed by the past, present, and future relationship of all things in all of time. Each choice is heavily swayed by variables beyond our control though it is made of our own free will.

Let's look at a pertinent example: Should I have written this book? Obviously, I chose to do so. And, some would say, I had free choice in the matter, voluntarily foregoing alternative endeavors. Others would say my decision was "meant to be," an evolutionary event whose time had come. Both positions have merit. Certainly, an Omniscient God would have anticipated my choice, being intimately familiar with my every thought, propensity, and inclination.

I suggest you are reading this because your life flow caused you to read it. I wrote this because my life flow led me to it. Could I have chosen to write something else? I could have, but I probably wouldn't have. Even though I had a choice, I suspect I would have chosen this path. The events that led to this writing and reading are so complex and interconnected that the final intersection of people, places, and time is beyond comprehension. The chain of events leading to this moment goes back indefinitely. Our timing is no fluke. You and I were channeled into this connection since forever. I don't know about you, but that makes me feel very special. This moment results from an incredible matrix of interrelated events. These events occur on a timeless universal scale, *always known* by God, but a consequence of our free choice.

The point is that each and every moment brings forth similar "accidental" or "coincidental" events, ripe for experience. Each apparently serendipitous happening is the product of innumerable previous choices and events. Everything that happens in this moment affects the next moment and the moment after that, ad infinitum. And yet, it is entirely contained simultaneously in an all-encompassing eternal moment. Is there room in that eternal moment for randomness?

If the Divine Universe is God experiencing Itself, it seems plausible that an Omniscient Being, knowing everything, including how we will choose and all of the probable outcomes, might allow us to make free-will choices so as to embellish Its experience in a so-called random way. Our choices and outcomes would be known but not controlled. However, they would always be consistent with the *already-existing* web of all that is. I call it dynamic free choice within a larger, all-encompassing, but known, eternal moment. It is kind of like swimming in a fishbowl – we are free to swim any which way we like, but the way we swim never changes the constraints of the bowl.

I'm sure the thought of having questionable control resulting from free-will choices will make some Las Vegas card counters very uncomfortable. But, do we really control things? We credit smart choices when things go our way. When things go wrong, we blame fate. Ultimate control is extremely questionable. So, what is our incentive to make advantageous choices?

Advantageous choices enable us to grow in a positive way. Living an ethical existence is self-rewarding. Following our innate moral compass enhances the quality of our life experience. Inner peace is the goal. Once attained, nothing else matters.

This selfish motive has a more attractive sister: helping others. What goes around comes around. It's a win-win formula with an exponential effect.

Can we be a successful bank robber, living a plush life at the expense of others, and experience true joy? I think not. The best a successful bank robber can hope for is shallow, short-term comfort. Negative choices that harm others go against our basic Divinity, personally and collectively, hindering our spiritual progress.

There is a growing body of contemporary thought regarding the phenomenon of an evolutionary force or universal flow toward enhanced spiritual awareness. The thinking is that universal energy demonstrates a historical propensity to progress from simple forms to more complex forms, thereby facilitating evolutionary development. As evolution advances to more complex biological forms, as in humans, we become sentient, experiencing an increased capacity for awareness of spiritual connection, a guided journey toward the ethics of truth, love, and beauty. Universal flow toward greater spiritual awareness is the key to a better world. When we talk about "being in the flow," perhaps we are subconsciously expressing recognition of our efforts within that guiding force, a sense of participation in its collective spiritual current.

> *Is it productive to swim upstream? That's what we do when we try to force things to happen. Isn't it more satisfying to allow the current to carry us to where we should be? Of course, initiative and planning have their place—but only if we take the right path. When we're on that path or "with the flow," we experience a certain ease and confidence in tomorrow. We start going around obstacles rather than over them. The idea of disappointment melts away as we accept what comes along. It gets easier*

for us to appreciate and understand our connection to everything and everyone around us. We no longer live our lives separate and apart from everything and everyone else. We allow our lives to unfold, realizing that we may never comprehend or control all of this. And, we come to enjoy and rely on a certain comfort in fulfilling our purpose.

Then, how do we go about making the most advantageous choices? The secret is to listen to our spiritual energy. We evaluate alternatives, and make choices in different ways. The decision-making process can take place in the mind or from a deeper source, our intuition. When we use our minds to make choices, we unavoidably involve our value system, which is judgmental and can distort the real truth. Our minds further complicate things by playing to the perceived requirements of our egos, such as the need for acceptance, recognition, power, and success. Those needs often conflict with spiritual needs, resulting in superficial, transient pleasure rather than true joy. By following our intuition or "gut feeling" we make more advantageous choices. Intuitive feelings come from *Being*. These feelings are a more reliable compass on our journey to experience the highest possible connection. Intuitive messages are not warped or filtered through worldly experience, as are the messages of the mind. Instead, they tap into our Divine Energy. For example, artists draw on intuitive energy for their creativity. Ideally, artists connect with their inner self and let their art flow from that source, uninterrupted by the mind. Some artists are more creative than others because it is easier for them to make that connection and keep it open. The same wellspring is constantly available to all of us.

It is helpful to differentiate between superstition and intuition. Superstition is an unjustified belief in the supernatural causation of an event. Intuition is the power, without conscious thought, to understand an event. Superstition obstructs truth. Intuition taps into it. You *may* walk under a ladder if it feels right!

Listening to our sixth sense provides the best source for making life's decisions. Our intuition will guide us toward the highest choices. Some of the messages come from within. By being aware, we can recognize internal messages and act upon them. We may be searching for an answer in prayer or meditation, or the thought may occur in a dream. The trick is to recognize the message. It helps to meditate and check in with our spirit or inner self on a regular basis.

Some intuitive signs come from the outside world. All of us have experienced absolutely improbable events that we conveniently call "coincidences," or "accidents." Often, these so-called coincidences have a profound effect on the direction of our lives. For example, who hasn't been surprised to meet a friend from the past, and, arising out of that improbable meeting, experienced a change in their lives? Or, by that most unlikely intervention, been influenced to pursue things in an entirely different way?

I would like to share a "coincidence" that's close to home. Several years ago, when I was drafting my first paper on the Divine Universe, I went to a Stephen Hawking book for information on the relativity of time. I had read the book years before, and anticipated having a difficult time locating the necessary information. As I sat by a sunny window, the book fell open on my lap, exposing two pages. It just so happens, I had a prism resting on the adjacent window frame so that, as the sun changed position, I could enjoy a rainbow of light moving across the room. Much to my surprise, at the very instant the book opened, the prism directed a beam of sun light onto the needed paragraph. Was that just a coincidence or was it a sign? The probability of the exact page being open at the exact time, and the position of the sun in relation to the prism highlighting that paragraph, has to be infinitesimally small. Was that a random event or could it have been encouragement to continue?

There are no coincidences or accidents. We just misinterpret them as such. They are external signs that affect our choices. Developing awareness allows us to recognize these signs and use them to make positive improvement. However, life experiences can interfere with or diminish that sensitivity.

We are a competitive culture. As children, we are taught to progress and excel without regard for our inner self. As adults, we measure success in terms of ownership and power. Little time is devoted to feeling the flow of things and the quiet peacefulness of being in tune with our Life Force. Because of it, our culture is filled with anxious musicians, unfulfilled industrialists, sad celebrities, insincere leaders, and shallow consumers. In our run for the roses, we forget to smell them. Instead, we rush right by or trample one of the great truths: our Life Force will show us the way. All we need is a present awareness and the conviction to trust our feelings.

Choices are guided by values. Are we capable of realizing ethical behavior without the morality of religion? What is the hierarchy of authority in a Divine Universe? To properly consider these issues, we must examine the basis of all order, natural law.

CHAPTER 5
Natural Rights

Waskal Wabbit

Rabbit, a.k.a. "Wiggles," was brought in for trial
Not really fitting your criminal profile
Accused as a trespasser, and caught before dark
All Wiggles had done was eat clover in the park

With no way of knowing he'd committed a crime
They inked him and footprinted one paw at a time
Photos revealed long teeth stained dark green
Witnesses wrote down the munching they'd seen

Judge "Charley" Possum called his filled court to order
While casting a glance at the cute court reporter
Poor Wiggles was dragged to the cold witness box
By his longtime nemesis, Sheriff "Wiley" Fox

Municipal lawyers claimed well-informed trespass
Because of a sign that said, "STAY OFF THE PARK GRASS"
Wiggles testified in his beleaguered defense
Saying this law was contrary to all common sense

Denying rabbits clover is unjust deprival
Of basic foodstuff that they need for survival
Multiply as they may, it would hardly be enough
If they didn't have access to green three-leaved stuff

Judge Possum's gold glasses slid down on his nose
As an unexpected shuffle and clamor arose
When Wiggles half shouted, "This law is unfair;
'Cause it tramples the natural rights of a hare!"

At that, Wiggles feared of his instant removal
Though the court reporter winked her tacit approval

In favor of defendant, the case was concluded
"Should never have been brought," Judge Possum alluded

With prosecutors warned to cease and desist
Any and all charges were quickly dismissed
Wiggles, relieved that the whole thing was over
Went back to a life of eating sweet clover

And, a higher law prevailed. . . .

Natural rights provide the inalienable authority that we possess by virtue of our very existence or *Being*. These rights are neither subservient nor subject to any human laws or rules. They are the highest order of authority, deriving their preeminence from our Divine Nature. Natural rights include the right to life, liberty, equality, well-being, and death. Any regulation of human behavior must yield to and respect natural rights. Any law or rule in violation of natural rights is invalid for lack of authority.

The question arises, if everything in the universe is Divine, what are the relative natural rights of humans? As the dominant species, we tend to think that we have natural rights over all things. Our view of human domination is colored by a heavy creationist influence in our culture, whereby humans are thought of as the only life form capable of spirituality. Because of this, we tend to think of ourselves as the chosen species. In a Divine Universe all things, not just humans, have natural rights, because all things are made of the same Divine Energy. How then can we reconcile that fact with our own needs for survival and well-being?

It is fair to assume that *Being* inherently includes the need of all species to pursue survival and perpetuation. The spiritual aspect of all things is affected by consumption preference in the survival food chain. We choose how and what to consume based on our needs and ability to satisfy those needs.

Dominant species have a duty to minimize loss of life and waste. We are responsible for regulating consumption in a way that allows for the greater benefit of all things.

In the everyday world, our survival ethic should be to take no more than we reasonably need. One of our greatest responsibilities, after self-preservation, is to protect and preserve the world around us, realizing that all things are Divine. This necessarily includes deciding which plants and animals will live or die. Our present consciousness should include a regular evaluation of what is truly necessary for living, and how those needs affect everything else. Our choices should show respect for the natural rights of subservient species and our frugal governance of their environment.

> *Food is necessary for survival and should be consumed with concern for the greater benefit of all things. Questioning the food choices we make allows for efficient and respectful consumption. For example, by consuming large quantities of meat, we encourage less efficient use of resources and show a lack of respect for subservient species. Because most cattle are no longer range fed, it takes three to seven pounds of grain to raise one pound of beef. That extra grain could have fed a hungry child. Did we make the highest choice when we ate beef for dinner? Overharvesting of our oceans is a direct result of our failure to connect. With an awareness of the Divinity of all things, we avoid polluting our air and water. Pouring drain oil into a sewer is like pouring it into our own mouths. Wasting resources by building huge houses for small families, and driving large, inefficient vehicles show a lack of environmental responsibility. By recognizing Universal Divinity, we enhance the quality of our lives*

and promote the betterment of all that is, definitely a win-win proposition.

Sensitivity in these matters is greatly increased if we develop and use our present consciousness. The most advantageous choices come easily to those who have a constant awareness of the shared Divinity of the universe and the natural rights of all things. Those natural rights form the basis for the evolution of today's ethics and rules.

CHAPTER 6
Ethics and Rules

Conflict

A happy young man, I was footloose and free
Having nothing but love in my eye
'Till the padre arrived with a message for me:
Change your ways and repent 'fore you die

Shun everything evil; embrace what is good
Always follow the straight-narrow way
It was something worthwhile I'd do if I could
But much better tomorrow than today

At midnight the devils and angels would gather,
Causing mayhem at the foot of my bed
Feathers and pitchforks, blood, sweat, and lather
First forward, then back, I was led

At some point I cried out, "Enough is enough!"
And I told them as never before
My conscience is poisoned with judgmental stuff
Then showed good and evil the door
Fear of God, nevermore . . .

Long before organized religion, early man gazed at the stars above the African savanna and pondered the inevitable questions: Who am I? Why am I here? Where did I come from? What is my purpose? What happens to me when I die? We had evolved to a level of self-realization, allowing us to appreciate great mysteries and to search for answers in someone or something more intelligent than ourselves, the spiritual world.

As our search evolved, man sought to organize beliefs by entrusting them to knowledgeable, devout individuals who spent their days formalizing spiritual ideas and ministering to the transcendental needs of the tribe. The day of the shaman marked the birth of religion. Since then, religious beliefs have been woven into the fabric of our lives.

Most major religions are based on the life of a significant spiritual leader along with related scripture containing written laws or rules. These leaders and their scripture have had a profound historical influence on modern values. Teachings based on evolving doctrine and tradition served as guidelines and became the code for ethical behavior. With respect for its prior usefulness, today's evolved moral code should be measured for relevancy and propriety just as we examine any other part of contemporary life.

Current moral values include a lot of questionable baggage. It is useful to examine the religious concepts that fostered them to understand their basis and how they motivate behavior. Though religions vary in form, they contain—not surprisingly—similar foundational leaders, concepts, and a rather universal pattern of behavioral control. The predominant control system necessitates viewing the world in terms of "good" and "evil." The basic premise of this system is that people are inherently weak, spiritually. They are subject to negative influence by dark or evil forces. Evil forces are characterized to be in constant conflict with the forces of good to control human willpower. In this system, submission to the temptation of evil results in failure to lead a good life and warrants some appropriate form of spiritual punishment. Forgiveness can only come through institutionally sanctioned redemption in which the religious institution acts as an intermediary between the sinner and God. God is thought of as outside the physical realm, separate and apart from all things. The thrust is to encourage people to make the right choices for fear of God. If you are good, God will love and reward you. If you are bad, God will punish you. This judgmental God is often presented as vindictive and vengeful, creating natural disasters such as floods and plagues to punish sinners. Practically speaking, a system of good and evil enables organized religion to maintain control over members through fear.

Religious rules regarding right and wrong extend to obligations based on institutional doctrine. These internal doctrines expand control over followers by requiring that doctrinal directives be obeyed. For example, many religions teach that theirs is the only true religion and that anyone outside that religion cannot be redeemed. And many religious doctrines condone discrimination against women and gay people by restricting or prohibiting their participation. In ways such as these, doctrine also influences moral values.

I have met many well-intentioned, institutionally religious people working for the betterment of mankind. Nevertheless, it's hard to ignore the fact that religion also has a business side. Institutional religions, consistent with the nature of formal bureaucracies, place a high priority on perpetuating themselves. They have every incentive to maintain their position as a spiritual intermediary through scripture and doctrine. They present themselves as necessary authorities on evil. Any goodness is channeled through them. This closed system directly affects our lives and how we perceive our world. Behavioral control through fear of God is responsible for a great deal of negativity in our society today. But an alternative exists.

What if we're always connected to God and don't need an intermediary? What if we're quite capable of leading an ethical life outside the concept of good and evil?

Here is a thought that will change your life forever: Good and evil do not exist! With God as the universe, *It* cannot be good or evil, It just *is*. Good and evil are religious moral concepts founded on the premise that God is separate and apart from a sinful universe. When we get past that notion, a whole new way of thinking opens up. No more living in fear of the dark side. Every day becomes a positive spiritual experience. Pain and suffering are no longer "punishment," but rather just another aspect of being human.

> *A marvelous thing happens when we remove fear of God from our daily lives: We no longer see ourselves as sinners, but rather as joyful participants experiencing who we are as a part of God. We no longer see ourselves as good or bad. Instead, we think of ourselves as fallible human beings trying to elevate our spirituality by making advantageous choices. We become motivated by love, not fear. And, that makes all the difference!*

But, what about people like Adolf Hitler? Wasn't he evil, having sent millions of innocent people to their graves?

Even people like Adolf Hitler share in the spiritual matrix of Divine Energy. Therefore, they cannot be inherently evil. Rather, they fail to recognize their Divinity and make choices that harm others. Our natural right of survival gives us the authority to take necessary measures to protect against such threats. Some would argue that protection justifies taking life. Others would argue that taking life is never justified. I reason that taking any life, human or otherwise, is contrary to the concept of Universal Divinity, and would be justified only in extreme circumstances, where no other course of action is feasible. Regardless, we are all spiritually connected, even to the people we dislike. When we look in the mirror, they are included in our image. What we do to another person, we do to ourselves. The realities of life present difficult spiritual decisions. It is far too easy to label someone inherently evil. Our judgment must be guided and tempered by a consciousness of the Divinity of all things. Which leads to a logical question,

Are we capable of forming an ethical code without religion and its moral system of good and evil?

Let's return, for a moment, to our primitive ancestors on the savannas of Africa, long before the advent of organized religion. It seems reasonable that survival was the defining feature of day-to-day life. (Some would say the same applies today and that only the jungle has changed—it's now a crowded city and urban sprawl!) Decisions were made that promoted successful survival, first for the individual, and then for the family or extended clan. Though we probably didn't think about it, our natural right to life was the basic authority for our actions. It's not much of a stretch to imagine that, early on, we realized that if you wanted good things for yourself, you had to treat others as you expected them to treat you. In small hunter-gatherer groups, helping outsiders resulted in enhanced security, resource sharing, and enlarged mating selection. And so, the cornerstone of all social behavior was set, probably for self-serving reasons. The ethic was simple: Wherever possible, treat others fairly because it enhances successful survival and the quality of your own life. On this foundation arose the structure of civilization: family relations, rules for ownership and distribution of property, government, liberty, equality, and justice. These ideals evolved out of inherent natural rights and, most probably, because of their stand-alone character, would have developed in the ordinary course of sentient evolution with or without religion. It appears that we've been marching toward a truthful ethic since day one. And it's debatable whether the moral system of good and evil has hindered more than it has helped. Our standards or ethics are a constantly evolving guide, subject to contemporary evaluation and improvement. The theory of good and evil should be subjected to the same scrutiny.

Religious tradition has woven good and evil into the heart of our culture. A case in point: heads of state arbitrarily labeling certain foreign countries "evil empires." The thrust of such a statement is one of religious judgment, not civil criticism, and goes beyond ethics. It implies that our enemies are on the spiritual dark side, an undeniable imposition of our religious beliefs under the guise of ethics. The inference is that our political agenda should prevail because God favors us. The example illustrates how the concept of "morality" is mistaken as a measurement of ethical behavior. Moral righteousness allows us to rationalize the destruction of our "evil" enemies. It also shows how a code of ethics is less objective when tainted with religious beliefs. In a Divine Universe, our code of ethics evolves directly from our connection with God and is based on natural rights. Because of that Divinity, evil does not exist.

Religious doctrines are based on the premise that God is good. Of course, we don't know that to be a fact. A good, nurturing, loving God is how we have chosen to construct Its image. But, what if God isn't necessarily "good"? Would a loving God allow innocent children to suffer and die in natural disasters? Would a loving God condemn people for choices that are foreseeable? What if God is indifferent about how It experiences Itself? Does that mean there is no love or concern for us? Obviously, I don't have answers to these questions because any scenario is possible. Logically, I favor a God of goodness because of our apparent evolution toward ethical truth. We are moving in the direction of universal awareness. I find it reasonable that our human progress is a reflection of, and evidence of, our connection in the greater goodness of a Divine Universe. Beyond that, I can only say God "just is." To expect any more or less, in human terms, is to entertain folly.

That leaves us with a code of ethics based on our shared Divinity (i.e., natural rights and a God that may or may not care about us). Is it possible to enjoy inner peace and contentment without all of the answers? Let's look at human spirituality and how awareness can help.

CHAPTER 7
Human Spirituality

Generation

Feel our Life Force flow
From primordial-fresh slime
To the present time

There are several major theories of spiritual origin.
The Creation Theory, or its latest incarnation, Intelligent Design, proposes that God created humans, separate and apart from all other things, and gave them exclusive spirituality or a soul.

The Divine Intervention Theory proposes that all things evolved from common elements but at some evolutionary point, God intervened and gave humans exclusive spirituality.

The Non-Spiritual Evolution Theory proposes that humans evolved as a part of an ongoing universal process that is not influenced by any Fundamental Being and is purely a natural phenomenon.

Lastly, the Spiritual Evolution Theory proposes that humans evolved from common universal elements in a universe that *is* God, and, as a consequence, the universe and humans have always been spiritual.

Creationists believe that only humans are spiritual (have a soul) and that nothing else is spiritual. This theory raises many difficult questions regarding how you define "human." Were Neanderthals human, and did they have spirituality? What about other evolutionary lines that branched out from humans? How do we distinguish between humans and other highly developed mammals? If we use mental or emotional development as our yardstick, what is the defining level of intelligence? With the strong probability that life exists in outer space, at what point, if at all, would that life be considered human and be spiritual? Are unborn humans (fetuses) spiritual? Defining "human" leaves much to be desired and leaves us without a litmus test.

The Theory of Divine Intervention is troublesome in much the same way. At some point in time man alone would have been instilled with a spirit and that raises the same "human" definition problems as the Creation Theory. Besides, how do we know that God cares to intervene? And why would a Deity have to go back and correct or embellish Its own work?

The Spiritual Evolution Theory and the Non-Spiritual Evolution Theory are consistent with scientifically proven facts regarding Earth's origin (i.e., all things evolved from the same cosmic dust containing the same universal energy). That still leaves us with the question of whether universal evolution embodies a Prime Mover or God. If we believe it does, then a logical consequence is the spiritual interrelationship of all things.

As humans evolved and developed an awareness of *Being*, there came a time when they began to recognize and appreciate their spirituality. They came to realize, *I am!* Evolving humans placed food, clothing, and other travel-related objects in burial tombs, evidencing a belief that the deceased's spirit would journey to another life, and that it would transcend the physical body. Their spiritual beliefs were reflected in art that deified nature. It was not unusual for ancient cultures to worship the Earth, Sun, or Moon. Many cultures believed that the environment was a sacred extension of their personal spirituality. Native Americans recognized a spiritual obligation to preserve and protect their environment for the benefit of all. They believed they were temporary earthly tenants connected to the land. They understood their spirituality as timeless, connecting them with their ancestors and successors. They knew all things were interrelated and that they shared a spiritual nature with everything around them. In a circa 1858 letter to the U.S. government, which I have paraphrased and selectively presented below, the American Indian Chief Seattle wrote of that connection:

> *The President in Washington sent word that he wishes to buy our land. But how can you buy or sell the sky? The land? The idea is strange to us. If we do not own the freshness of the air and the sparkle of the water, how can you buy them?*
> *... If we sell you our land, remember that the air is precious to us; that the air shares its spirit with all the life it supports. The wind that gave our grandfather his first breath also receives his last sigh. The wind also gives our children the spirit of life. So if we sell you our land, you must keep it apart and sacred, as a place where man can go to taste the wind that is sweetened by the meadow flowers.*
> *... Will you teach your children what we have taught our children? That the earth is our mother? What befalls the Earth befalls all of the sons of the Earth.*
> *... This we know: the Earth does not belong to man; man belongs to the Earth. All things are connected like the blood that unites us all. Man did not weave the web of life He is merely a strand in it. Whatever he does to the web, he does to himself....*

Human spirituality is the result of a direct connection with God. Our spiritual energy is separate and yet indivisibly a part of one Great Spiritual Energy. Because of this, we are connected to—and a part of—every other person's spirit. And because the entire universe is Divine, our spiritual connection extends to everything in—or out of—existence. That would include such things as the trees, sky, plants, animals, and even empty space. The true dimensions of this connection can be better understood in the context of Perpetual Time. Our spiritual connection with God extends through the past, present, and future to include all of our eternal existence in perhaps many universes. That is the true meaning of *Being*, or existing in the moment. We might then ask, why do we exist at all?

It seems reasonable that our energy has chosen to work through and experience a biological life. In the process, we become capable of choosing who we are and who we want to be. Each time we make advantageous choices, we progress to a higher level of spiritual consciousness. As our level of consciousness increases, it becomes easier for us to experience our Divinity. At the highest level, we become capable of experiencing pure joy or enlightenment.

In order to better understand the path to enlightenment, we must view it as a timeless spiritual evolution. Upon conception, male and female cells combine to form a new biological entity, complete with spiritual energy. Our spiritual energy always has and always will exist. It merely takes a new form, namely, us. By virtue of this biological-spiritual relationship, God is a part of our new being, connecting us in every way to the Divine Universe. From that moment on, we begin to create the world, as we perceive it.

If we believe everything in the universe is pure energy, it follows that we have the ability to shape our world by directing that energy. Early Greek philosophers proposed that the world doesn't exist in reality, but is merely a construction of our thoughts. In a Divine Universe of pure energy, that theory poses some fascinating possibilities. We know that energy can change form, such as a burning log that becomes ashes and smoke, or water that goes from solid ice to liquid, to steam. Thus, it is possible that the universe may exist only in our minds, with the energy of our perception, causing the world to take whatever form we wish. If that is the case, the universe we experience may be the universe that we choose to experience.

Whether we believe the world is real or imagined, we influence our personal world, our perceived reality, and our life's experience by directing universal energies.

Experiments in quantum physics reveal that minute particles such as electrons appear to change both direction and form when influenced by the presence/thoughts of an observer. Scientists now think of particles/wavelengths as "possibilities" rather than "matter" or "light," susceptible to behavioral changes induced by mental suggestion. These experiments indicate that we have great power to change our world by directing our energy for that purpose. We create our own reality by consciously choosing and redefining our experiences.

The world we perceive is a product of our choices and a reflection of who we are. Of course, some people are born into more favorable circumstances than others, but, regardless of our situation, the energy we set in motion shapes the world we've inherited and brings us the experiences we need to progress. There is no such thing as a good or bad experience, though some are obviously more pleasant than others. Each experience provides an opportunity to spiritually grow and to expand our self-awareness, regardless of life's circumstances.

Throughout our lives, our Energy continues to work within the world we perceive to bring us experiences that present choices for spiritual growth. How well we interpret experiences and make choices will determine how rapidly our spiritual growth progresses. This evolution can be accelerated if we work at developing our consciousness.

CHAPTER 8
Consciousness

Renewal

Did you feel the velvety wetness of the dew
Hear the pure joy in a robin's song
Sense the weight of warm moisture in your lungs
Perceive your purpose in things, on a larger scale
Smell the faint perfume of emerging lilacs
Feel the rub of your clothing
Notice the cautious opening of the morning flowers
See the street lights go off in such orderly fashion
Sense the connection of your movement to everything around you
Hear the background hum of traffic
Witness the renewal that comes with first light
Taste the smoky, sour pollution
Feel the soft breeze on your skin as it tickles your body hair
Hear the sound of your footsteps as your presence changes everything
Feel slightly sad for the last moths still circling the porch light
Notice the changing palate of colors in the sky
Smell the timelessness of the damp, fresh earth
Have an awareness of night creatures retreating into the shadows
See flowers with dormant insects, waiting for the warmth of our nearest star
Hear the rustle of green leaves as the wind comes to life?
Feel like you'd been here before. . . .

Present consciousness is an awareness of what is happening at the present moment undistracted by any thoughts about the past or future. It is also referred to as *Being*. People with an advanced present consciousness are keenly aware of everything and everyone around them. They focus intently on the presence of another, connecting physically and spiritually with undivided attention. They eat their food so that they focus on the taste of each and every bite. They don't just sit in a room, but feel the space. The smallest detail is noticed—and felt. They never allow distractions to divert their senses from focusing on the experience at hand. They choose this approach because they know that only the present exists, and that thoughts of the past or future dilute the present experience. In other words, they choose to live only in the present or now as intensely as possible. They realize that allowing their minds to be occupied with thoughts of the past or future steals the present moment from them. While, initially, this takes purposeful concentration, it eventually becomes second nature. It is all too human to worry about an important package that failed to go out yesterday or fret about tomorrow's dentist appointment. All we have is now. Our greatest loss is to fail to experience this very moment.

Developing a present consciousness requires persistent monitoring of our sensory perception and thought process. With present consciousness we are aware of each choice we make. *It is as if we are an outside witness observing our own choices.* The choices can be carefully measured to determine if they conform spiritually to who we are, and who we want to be.

For example, we may be offended by a manipulative friend's need to control. Without giving it thought, we might be judgmental and confrontational. But, having the benefit of present consciousness, we realize that being "right" and asserting our ego is not as important as allowing the other person to be comfortable. So, we ask ourselves, Who are we, and who do we want to be? Our choice will never be "right" or "wrong." Rather, it will be more or less spiritually advantageous. A productive choice would be to overlook the situation and develop a solution that doesn't hurt the other person's feelings. On the surface, it looks as if we have turned the other cheek. But beneath the surface, we have acted in our own best interest by preserving our inner peace, avoiding a no-win argument, and fostering goodwill. On a larger scale, we have chosen to act in the best interest of all things.

This advantageous choice elevates our spirituality, and reinforces the connection with our Divinity. It also provides a positive example for the other person. The resulting spiritual progress brings us a tiny bit of joy on the journey to enlightenment. As our present consciousness becomes stronger, we are much more aware of each choice at any given moment. Thus, a healthy, active, present consciousness is a critical tool.

Prayer and meditation are common methods for strengthening our level of consciousness. There is no right way. The preferred method is to set aside all worldly distraction, empty our minds, and enter into a state where we connect to our spirit with focus and intensity. An intermediary such as a religious institution can be used, but is not necessary. We already have everything we need within ourselves. The benefits of connecting are spiritual and physical. Connection helps to relax the body and relieve stress. It refreshes and renews. Most importantly, it gives us a sense of peace and joy, freeing our minds, and centering our being. Touching our Divine side energizes us with positive direction and clear priority. As we increase the frequency of our meditation or prayer, the connection gets easier, and the feeling becomes more intense. Eventually, connection is possible during our daily tasks without formal prayer or meditation.

Enlightenment is a high state of spiritual development that allows us to stay constantly connected to our Divine Energy. It may empower us to do things that are thought to be physically impossible. Though I have not personally witnessed such things, I keep an open mind because there appears to be credible evidence that they exist. Humans who reach enlightenment are often called Masters. Some suggest that the great religious figures were actually Masters of enlightenment. Others believe that the great religious figures had the power of Masters because they were God, or were so in touch with their God-self that they became God in surrogate. It is probable that all Masters experience an advanced degree of Universal Knowledge. This heightened connection with the spiritual and physical universe may allow them to perform "miracles" or accomplish things that have no worldly explanation. By directing energy, Masters may be able to heal people. Understanding and using Perpetual Time, they may be able to move in and out of the past, present, and future. This would allow them to be in two places at once, or disappear from the present. By controlling and directing their Divine Energy, they would be able to walk on water, levitate, or walk through walls. By allowing energy to change form, Masters would be capable of taking different forms, or returning to their own form after death. Whether we reach an enlightened state will depend on how far and how fast we spiritually evolve.

The spiritual energy that all of us possess is constantly active, and accessible. It is the Divine part of us that we often fail to recognize or appreciate. It is the same energy that Masters use today. We all have the ability to become Masters by elevating our level of spiritual awareness.

As we reach the end of our physical life, we are confronted with the spiritual ramifications of our demise. Death is the physical end of a biological life. Based on the testimony of previous generations we know that the universe existed before we were born, and will probably continue after our bodies die. Therefore, it is reasonable to assume that our spirit will survive death in some manner because we are a part of the Divine Universe. What happens to our Divine Energy after death? Some organized religions teach that we travel to be with God in a "heavenly," supernatural place, assuming that we make it through their version of "final judgment." These religions deem judgment necessary because they teach that we are sinners, separate from God, and must be redeemed. In a Divine Universe, we never leave God because we are a part of God. We were a part of God before we were conceived, while we are alive, and after we die. There is no need to be "reunited" with God in a place like "heaven." After death, our Divine Energy continues, lacking nothing. Our energy remains a separate but indivisible part of the whole energy, which is the Divine Universe. And, as we learned in science class, it seems logical that, if no energy is ever lost, our energy will continue in the universe in some other way.

Assuming our energy continues on after biological death, one of the intriguing mysteries is whether we would have consciousness (i.e., would we "know" that we exist?). In the event that we do have such an awareness, it would raise an interesting situation where all sentient beings from the past would join those of the present (and, perhaps the future) in a collective consciousness. Is it a coincidence that the whole idea brings us back to the concept of a timeless universe?

Collective or group consciousness is a phenomenon whereby a multitude of people, independently asserting consciousness in a common idea, become joined as one voice, focusing the power of that collective energy. The participants need not be gathered in the same place or even be aware that someone else has the same intention.

Collective consciousness is facilitated by a universal matrix of energy. Everything in the universe has energy and radiates that energy, animate and inanimate objects alike. The energy is constantly moving about, connecting with other energies, and changing form. This dynamic constantly affects us as it shapes our lives and the world around us. We are always connected but must develop a present consciousness to be aware of it. As we raise the level of present consciousness, our ability to tap into the energy of the universe intensifies. This connection provides us with great power. With the power of collective consciousness, our spiritual connection with the energy of the universe magnifies our ability to influence issues in the larger world.

Government policies on such things as the environment can be guided and changed through collective consciousness. If enough people in their spiritual consciousness direct energy for the purpose of protecting the rain forests, that positive energy will influence the policy makers, even though they may be unaware of it. Conversely, if apathy is widespread, policy makers will find it easier to promote special agendas contrary to the common good. For example, negative collective consciousness can have an indirect effect on natural phenomena such as cataclysmic weather by promoting poor environmental practices. Applying the rain forest example to global issues such as war and human rights, it is apparent that unsatisfactory government and its negative consequences stem from a lack of positive collective consciousness on these issues.

We live in a world where many people are still fighting for basic human rights, and where war remains an acceptable solution for disagreement. In an enlightened world, a collective consciousness will eliminate war and protect the natural rights of everyone. We should not underestimate the power of the energy that we send out.

Collective consciousness will take down barriers to global change. But, before that happens, we have to stop thinking of ourselves as separate nationalities in cities, states, or countries, and, instead, think of ourselves as one global, universal people, spiritually interrelated with common goals. Awareness of our commonality will allow a global consciousness to rise up and change the world so that people treat each other as they treat themselves. And ultimately, compassion, respect, and understanding will overcome selfishness, hatred, and ignorance.

CHAPTER 9
Conclusion

With God as the Universe, we are a part of a great matrix of Divine Energy that encompasses everything that is. Our life's experiences and the world in which we live are shaped by how we use that Energy. We exist in an eternal moment containing all of time, past, present, and future. Within that moment, we choose who we are and who we want to be, individually and collectively, respectfully observing the natural rights of all things. Our intuition and innate moral compass guide us on a spiritual journey to higher awareness, enhanced connection with our Divinity, and inner peace.

PART TWO
A Day in the Divine Universe

CHAPTER 10
First Light: Awakening

I open my eyes to the first light of day. The birds are singing, renewing their territorial claims. Thunder rumbles in the distance. My body says, "Don't go," but my mind and soul, says otherwise. After a few stretching exercises, I put on my running shoes and hit the pavement. Once I'm up and going, the reward is well worth the effort. A sense of connection stirs me as I coax cranky muscles into motion. I begin to experience another day in this fascinating drama called life. It is an experience of sights, sounds, and smells, all with the feeling of a new beginning—both ancient and immediate. I am a solitary runner, enjoying this introspective time—my psychiatrist's couch at a fraction of the cost.

As I sort through my thoughts, I sometimes find it necessary to rein in negativity. I do this by maintaining an awareness of my thought process. For instance, I may be following a mental thread regarding an anticipated family gathering, when I realize I will probably be stuck at a table with Uncle Bob, the know-it-all. The trick is to step outside the situation and be a witness to my own thoughts. Then, intervene to redirect things in a positive way. I choose an approach that will overcome any negativity. That night when I'm seated by him I will seize the moment when he says, "You know, that car of yours would get better mileage if it had larger wheels." To that, I'll say, "You're right, but it would get even better mileage if it were a friction-free hovercraft." Hopefully, the humor will help him to be aware of his know-it-all side without hurting his feelings, making the situation more manageable and enhancing my inner peace.

Returning to the moment, I renew my connection: the road beneath my feet, cool moist air on sweat running down my face, the hum of rush hour traffic, other people out walking, smells of breakfast somewhere, a hungry baby crying. As I hear the child's voice, I am struck by the analogy of birth to the start of a new day and how this day is really just a continuation of the previous day and a connection to the next day.

CHAPTER 11
First Light: Birth

In a timeless universe, birth is a continuation rather than a beginning. Though I prefer to avoid spiritual labels, some would call birth a reincarnation. I simply think of it as a biological experience within a larger eternal existence or *Being*.

The point at which we commence biological life is a subject of great controversy. I suspect that we commence "life" when we are capable of biological function, independent of the host mother. Spiritually, the embryo, being new mass, becomes unique Divine Energy at the moment of conception.

Perhaps the abortion debate would benefit if biological life were distinguished from spiritual existence. In a Divine Universe, biological life is a limited experience; spiritual existence is eternal.

I recently held a young child at a family gathering. The experience felt brand new, as if I had never held my own children or grandchildren. Isn't it curious how life becomes more precious as we get older? Maybe it's because we are too busy while raising our own children to step back and really feel the impact of their presence. The child I held was a human miniature in every respect. I couldn't help but marvel at such perfection. And, as we all do, I wondered who this person would become.

During the 1960s and 1970s, sociologists promoted a popular theory that we are a product of all of our learning—that we are an empty computer until we download experiences and store that information, thereby forming a personality.

That theory always sounded a hollow ring for me. Isn't it curious that an infant is capable of showing amusement? How do they know, at age two months, what's funny and what isn't? Sharp, sudden sounds startle them and cause alarm. They didn't have environmental exposure to learn that. Biologists say that infants are merely reacting instinctively as a result of millions of years of genetic programming. I see it in a different context. I see it as a child experiencing *Being*. I see a child reacting with pure joy, sadness, surprise, curiosity and fear without the biased filters of adulthood. And I see "instinct" as something larger than knowledge or heredity. It is our innate spiritual energy, quietly directing our lives. It is this sixth sense that guides our choices and enables life's purpose: to be who we wish to be. Awareness of that sixth sense is an important part of making advantageous choices, which leads me back to my morning run and a sudden change in the weather.

CHAPTER 12

First Light: Attitude

That distant clap of thunder has turned into a roaring downpour. My feet splash through the pooling water as I round the corner and head for home. I am thoroughly soaked and somewhat uncomfortable. I almost curse the rain but catch myself. You can only get so wet! I remind myself that the situation is neither bad nor good, but just *is*. *Because I am*, I have an opportunity to experience this change of events as I wish to perceive them. Stepping outside myself, I see a runner slogging along, looking like a drowned rat, water dripping from his nose, shoes swamped, and clothes stuck to his body. Is that comical or what? I *choose* to laugh rather than curse. Because of my choice, I accept the adversity, reminding myself that I am connected to, and a part of this event. The weather is no longer a detached annoyance but a friendly challenge to who I am and who I want to be. There is no right way. I'm reminded of a friend who finds it delightful to mow his lawn in the rain. I guess his glass is always half full.

I recently attended a party where I talked with three sisters who happened to be sitting next to each other. After an extended conversation, it was easy to make a comparison: they had very different attitudes about their world. One sister looked at her glass as half empty. Another sister looked at her glass as half full. And the third sister drank from the bottle! I saw pessimist, optimist, and realist sitting side by side. We are constantly remaking our world. How we see things is a matter of choice. The sisters chose how they wished to view their world.

Isn't it interesting that we often find people in dire straits able to experience some joy when many of us, with everything, are so unhappy? Numerous self-help books have been written on the power of positive thinking. There is much scientific evidence to indicate that we have the ability to influence events around us by how we project our energy. Remember how Grandma always said, "Be careful what you wish for"? She was wiser than we realized. She knew from life's experience that our attitude has significant impact on the course of things.

Even if we sometimes experience a helpless feeling, there is much we can do to make the experience agreeable. The secret is to accept what comes along. Go with the flow. Stay positive. Look up at the stars and appreciate our connection to a much larger picture, which leads to some thoughts on our relationship with the vast natural world we call home.

CHAPTER 13

Natural World: Cycles

Last summer, at a northern lake, I became fond of a young family of black ducks. Momma duck would lead her four ducklings up the shore and over to the house allowing me to feed them under her watchful eye. Initially, the ducklings looked like fuzzy tennis balls. They were so young that it was necessary to crumble Cheerios so that they could swallow them. Needless to say, they didn't stay small for long. As the days passed, I watched them grow. Eventually, they were eating from my hand—though this made momma duck rather nervous. It was interesting to watch their permanent feathers and colors evolve. And our relationship became quite personal.

Then, one day in late August, the ducks came by without their mother. At first, I found her absence somewhat disturbing. It took some time to accept the fact that the four ducklings were now adults and ready for their first migration. She wisely gave them their independence. Looking back, it was I who was still attached. They disappeared after that last feeding. Later in fall, as wing after wing of geese and ducks flew down the lake, I wondered if my little friends were among them, their migration reminding me of life's cycles.

Everywhere we look we see the interrelated, complex fabric of the physical world. Nothing is without connection. If all four survive, four new ducks mean a gain of two additional ducks after the parents die. Additional life means greater demand for food, water, and nesting space. That affects the existence of all other life directly or indirectly. And those considerations affect us. Likewise, every time we step on an ant, we alter the natural world in some way. That tiny change ripples through the entire system causing endless amended cycles. Here's an example of how it might work: less ants equate to less bird food; lack of bird food reduces the number of birds; less birds eating mosquitoes allow for a greater number of mosquitoes; more mosquitoes result in a greater probability of malaria; increased exposure causes a gifted political science student to contract malaria and die; because of his death, the world loses the potential of a great statesman; without that great statesman nuclear negotiations fail for lack of leadership; because of failed negotiations, nuclear war destroys civilization. So, watch where you walk!

Everything has its moment, including us. We appear as a tiny blip crossing the screen of existence, but we are important in our connection to everything else. We may not find a world-famous medical cure, but providing a kind word or gesture for someone in need may alter, in a positive way, his or her life and their state of *Being*. We are constantly impacting the flow of events. Understanding our state of *Being* is the first step in appreciating our physical impact on Mother Earth.

CHAPTER 14

Natural World: Footprints

From the time of our birth to the time of our death, we literally and figuratively create an indelible "footprint." This footprint is a history of our existence upon the Earth. It shows how we use our world while we are here. It shows our regard for our fellow man and whether we protect the earth's resources for future generations. In short, our footprint shows who we are. We must measure that footprint if we are to understand what can be done to improve our world and that measurement is all about the difference between "need" and "want."

There are questions we should ask ourselves. Do we need large gas-guzzling vehicles? Do we need huge houses for a family of four? Can we justify raising grain-devouring animals for meat? Do we need green, weed-free lawns badly enough to use toxic fertilizers, pesticides, and herbicides? Are there substitutes for rain forest furniture? Do we really need even half of our must-have electronic gadgets? And the list goes on. The underlying question is, can we justify bad practices such as these knowing the damage they cause? Is that the imprint we wish to leave? Is that who we want to be?

Even if we live in that big house, eat poorly, or fail to use energy-efficient cars, there are positive compromises that can be made. We can take advantage of a nice day and bicycle to the store. Or, we can turn off the air-conditioning, go outside, and enjoy a picnic in the park. We can take advantage of all of our space and invite someone less fortunate to join us for a holiday dinner. We can easily donate some of those forgotten toys to a charitable organization. And discarded plastic, glass, aluminum, and paper can be recycled.

We don't live *on* this Earth. We are a *part of it*. What we do to it, we do to our children, our grandchildren, and ourselves. Our world is all connected. If we are to cultivate a sustainable footprint, we must assume responsibility for our acts. Many of today's environmental practices clearly cause permanent damage. Much of that damage, for instance climate change, is indirectly related to such things as increasingly violent weather. That weather causes untold hardship. Which brings to mind a question: in a Divine Universe, how do we reconcile our spirituality with cataclysmic natural events?

CHAPTER 15

Natural World: Cataclysmic Events

Human history is punctuated with natural disasters. Recently, an Asian tsunami killed hundreds of thousands of people, including many innocent children. Some media personalities said the tsunami was God's punishment for our sins. Many people wondered, even if it wasn't a form of punishment, how a loving God could allow such a thing to happen.

In these difficult situations, we struggle to reconcile our spirituality with reality. A large part of the problem is that we persist in thinking of God as separate and apart from us. In a Divine Universe, we are inseparable from God. And we are connected to a tsunami and the suffering of its victims. The best we can do is accept the fact that there may be no answer or reason. It is neither good nor bad, but just is. Obviously, we don't have all of the pieces to the puzzle. Perhaps our insistence on measuring God in human emotional terms is uninformed. The need to see God as loving, caring, and protecting is merely self-serving. Likewise, thinking God is vengeful, punishing, and vindictive is illogical, attributing human failings or weakness to a Deity and seating us in the same old "sinner's" pew, steeped in guilt.

Consistent with a Divine Universe, I suggest a more rational, productive approach: appreciate that, in spite of even the darkest consequences of natural disaster, our spirit will continue. Reminding ourselves of our Divinity removes fear from the equation. Reach out to the victims, as if we were one of them because we are—connected in every way. Accept the notion that the event is part of a complex web that we might never understand, and move beyond that point as quickly as possible. There is no justification for wasting the present moment.

It would be prudent to ask ourselves if ecological damage contributes to some environmental disasters and whether we can make lifestyle changes that might help. For instance, global warming appears to be the catalyst for more frequent and severe storms. It also appears to affect changes in where rain falls. When we play cowboy/cowgirl in our tank-sized Hummers, do we realize the connection between our tailpipe and starving children in the recently arid sub-Sahara? If each Hummer came with the picture of a starving child embossed on the dashboard, would that personalization help us feel the effect of our negligence?

The problem is as close as our backyard. Our children and grandchildren have a right to enjoy the benefits of clean water. They have a right to expect that we will leave them with clean air and a quality life. Will we measure up?

Our natural environment cannot be ignored. Directly or indirectly, it affects our everyday lives. Catastrophes are often dramatic indication of what needs attention. Our quality of life is dependent on our relationship with nature. That relationship will affect our interrelationship with all other things, including friends and family.

CHAPTER 16
Relationships: Family

Recently, I attended a family graduation party. It was as close as our family will get to another family reunion. There are now so many family members including cousins and second cousins that you would have to be a suicidal masochist to have the event at your house!

I'm sure most of us can relate to this scenario: less-mobile or immobile elderly seated at a long table passing judgment on today's culture; young, athletic teens engaged in heated physical competition on the lawn; the host and hostess dealing with one crisis or another, trying to make the event enjoyable; new babies being passed about and admired; middle-agers moving around and socializing—collecting the most recent family gossip; teenagers keeping an eye out for a hot friend-of-a-friend. In short, this could be a poster child for any-family U.S.A.

And so, I sit back, observe, and reflect on my gene pool. I've seen better, I've seen worse! Hollywood wouldn't be interested in us as the perfect family. But this is my extended family to which I belong and love dearly.

As I frame the larger picture, I see my extended family in constant transition, from young to old. I'm starting to feel like a history book as I struggle to remember the names and relationships of the children of children of cousins with whom I used to play when families visited on Sunday afternoons. That's right, families actually used to visit (during the Paleolithic era, before television)! The adults would drink and play cards while the kids ran around and got sick on sneaked soda pop. Feeling my own mortality, I look for ways to be a positive influence on the younger generation.

My other observation concerns our DNA line. The common thread is blood—Grandpa's bulbous nose, Grandma's sweet tooth, and that saying about the acorn never falling far from the tree. Family is the level where universal connection is most noticeable. I remind myself that the connection extends to all people and things, throughout the universe—a far more profound sort of bloodline, a common Divinity. But at the heart of it all are our parents and siblings. Our influence on children and grandchildren will be our truly lasting legacy.

CHAPTER 17
Relationships: Children

It is 10:00 a.m. in the morning as I reflect on my childhood experiences and how family affected them. It was around this time of morning that we would pack up and leave for our family vacations. I would count down the days prior to departure and make a list of things to bring. There was a sense of togetherness as Mom would prepare travel food, Dad would get the car ready, and siblings would pack and talk about things to do while on the road. It was a family adventure. In retrospect, the real magic was in being together, not in where we went. The vacation was merely a catalyst. We were exploring our relationship to each other.

Our initial value system comes from family. It is a system that we trust and use until we accumulate enough experience to form our own values. These early experiences should include the comfort of spiritual belonging. Children need to know that God is in them and a part of everything around them. An awareness of being spiritually connected gives them a secure basis from which to handle difficult situations. As children move from their preschool years and begin questioning those values, they place far more weight on our actions than our words. No adult ever sensed hypocrisy or insincerity as quickly as a child. Our actions will confirm our thoughts and choices. Do we practice what we preach? Inquisitive, young, measuring minds will test our values. They will know if we really believe in the values that we ask them to adopt.

Grandparents can be an important influence on children in their formative years. They bring wisdom that comes from age and experience. They enjoy the advantage of distance from the immediate family. Their detachment gives them an "expert-from-out-of-town" preferred status. Because of their position and extended experience, grandparents are uniquely situated to reinforce family values. This influence can be especially important during transitional years when a child begins to place more emphasis on peer groups rather than parents.

I had a close relationship with my maternal grandfather. He had a small farm that I would visit on weekends. As a young teenager, I helped him in his gardens and in the woods. When we weren't busy, I wandered off on my own to explore the beauty of the place. At night we had an unspoken tradition of not using electric lights. Instead, we would sit by lantern light. He would tell outrageous stories, the same ones he had told a thousand times, but each time with a slightly different twist. I never tired of those stories and was taken in by his sense of humanity. We talked with a candor and freedom that would have been impossible with my parents, through no fault of theirs. And we easily bridged the extended generation gap. We experienced a certain magical connection that gave me important footing in an uncertain adolescent world. To this day, I think of his simplicity when I have to sort through things. His compassion still inspires me.

After childhood, relationships outside the family become more significant. They are complex and challenging. Our success in these matters depends heavily on the value system that we carry forward. This is a time when we examine our moral compass. Values that don't ring true have to be adjusted or discarded to enable uninhibited spiritual and emotional growth. One of the first challenging experiences is feeling affection for someone outside the family.

CHAPTER 18
Relationships: Love

I have always been amused with the concept of romantic love. It can be so strong that it causes people to risk their lives. I wouldn't be foolish enough to profess an understanding of its powers. I leave that to more daring poets and deranged intellectuals. But I do have a curious question: Could it be a mystical connection? Is that why it's so magical? Could it be a time when we touch on our Divinity?

Though many years have passed, and I've traveled many roads, I have never forgotten my first love. It was a feeling like no other. She was young and vulnerable. I was the same age but much less mature. We would secretly meet at the local movie house and sit in the last row. The ushers usually turned a blind eye on necking as long as you stayed out of the way. We wore love bracelets (when our parents weren't around), with the two bracelet halves cut in an uneven way from the same piece of ornamental metal. We vowed to love each other until the end of time. Predictably, the intensity of our affection faded. Just as sand castles get washed out to sea, our romantic relationship lacked the necessary foundation to endure.

Romantic love is feel-good infatuation, not to be confused with a lasting or enduring love. Romantic love doesn't last because it is based on the faulty premise that loving someone will bring us love in return and that that reflected love would enable us to love ourselves. It may eventually evolve into enduring love, but usually fails because it requires obligation and is filled with expectation. In addition, sooner or later, it lets you know that you must be happy with yourself before you can love anyone else.

Enduring love is built on a foundation of self-love. Being reasonably satisfied with who we are, we freely engage in a relationship to share our person and our spiritual nature, expecting nothing in return. We see the relationship as an opportunity for mutual exchange to better understand who we are and progress toward who we want to be. Enduring love arises out of a relationship that requires neither obligation nor expectation. Rather, it respects the partner's needs and gives him or her freedom to grow, demonstrating selfless affection.

Love often leads to a voluntary formal union between two or more people called marriage; though many involuntary, arranged marriages, in which the parties hardly know each other, blossom into lifelong, loving relationships. And it must be acknowledged that some cultures structure their marriages as polygamous institutions. Then, there are other variations such as marriage of same-sex partners, and open marriages where, by agreement, the parties allow sex outside the relationship. Aside from any religious beliefs, there are many ways to make a formal commitment, with varying degrees of success.

We should be open to new ideas in view of the fact that 50 percent of all traditional marriages fail. We can readily see why that happens. They are based on historical, cultural, and religious obligations and expectations. Add to that, romantic love, and you have a dependable recipe for disaster.

I recently attended a traditional marriage ceremony. As I listened to the recitation of the parties, I was reminded of how challenging those promises were. Here stood two young people in their twenties, hardly having lived life, overcome by the temporary insanity of romantic love, vowing extraordinary commitments to each other. We all stood witness hoping for more than could be expected. Any court would have declared the proceedings void for lack of mental ability by the parties. Basing a formal union on personal freedom sounds contrary but might be a more successful approach.

Ironically, in the joining of two people, emphasis on freedom of self is an important ingredient for success. Certainly the parties need to work at the mutual aspects of a relationship such as compromise and affection. But, the primary focus should be on allowing each other the greatest latitude to make favorable spiritual choices. Then, being personally fulfilled, they can share their spiritual and physical lives in an open atmosphere of kindness, consideration, and trust. These ideas are the cornerstone of a lasting relationship and an enduring love.

The practical side of any formal relationship deserves attention. There are many new and constructive ideas for increasing the probability of success. Among them are compatibility tests, classes covering such things as sexuality, family planning, child rearing, career evaluation, financial planning, handling extended family and in-law friction, and religious differences. Finally, the partners might want to live together before marriage to test things out. The old-fashioned prolonged engagement still serves a useful purpose—exposing the parties to the realities of their relationship while allowing time for romantic notions to subside.

A spiritually based relationship can be effective with heterosexual partners, same-sex partners, or multiple partners, and it can work with or without sex. Which brings us to one of the great distortions and taboos of Western culture—sex.

CHAPTER 19

Relationships: Sex

Each camp says, "You can't live with them, and you can't live without them." Yet, we increase in numbers. Apparently, in our own bumbling way, we continue to find each other in the dark. I've heard it said that sex is God's bad joke. There may be some truth in that. Men are driven to secure sex. They spend their lives satisfying that drive, providing for their families, grinding themselves down. Women give up their looks and ruin their bodies bearing children, raising them, trying to put life in harmony. Most men and women end up sexless and unattractive because of physical deterioration at a time when they still need sex. In other words, in an indirect way, fulfilling this basic need eventually destroys us. I find that outcome to be comically ironic. Let's hope we never lose the ability to laugh at ourselves because we are a funny lot!

I happened to view a documentary about a group of "primitive" humans who had no previous contact with "civilized" culture. These people had a healthy concept of their sexuality. They were warm and loving—comfortable with public displays of affection. They enjoyed close contact and found it easy to touch each other. They accepted the aging process, and had no inhibitions about the decline of their bodies. There was no shame in being naked at any age. Sex was treated naturally and was openly discussed—often in good humor. The comfort level of their sexuality indicated a consciousness of spirit and an appreciation of the spiritual interrelationship of things. It was directly related to an open, uninhibited attitude. Yet, after discovering them, the first thing we did was to send in missionaries to convert them from their "pagan" ways! Perhaps our "civilized" view of sex is its own worst enemy.

In Western culture, present-day sexual mores are influenced by historical religious teachings. Probably arising out of an early need for family order and protection, social rules evolved that were eventually encoded in religious institutions. Institutions used those rules to influence and control members' sexual activities. In furtherance of their own purposes, they dictated how large families should be, and what sort of sexual behavior was appropriate. Because of the good/evil boogeyman, sex has evolved from a naturally beautiful experience into one tainted with fear, guilt, and inhibition. Fear of spiritual punishment has been used to control sexuality, setting forth what is sinful and what is not. In the process, a puritanical notion of sex permeates our society whereby strict requirements of conduct have produced sexual distortion and inhibition.

This perception is evident in the way that open conversation about sex, especially unconventional sex, is discouraged as "inappropriate." It thus becomes an uncomfortable subject that is avoided. Parents are reluctant to display affection in the company of their children. Children are taught to be ashamed of their nakedness. Sexual activity is only "appropriate" for procreative purposes, and any nonprocreative pleasure is frowned on.

I recently watched a popular travel show on public television. As the travel guide walked through a museum, I noticed that the genital areas in the famous human-form paintings were being blurred out. At the end of the program, the host mentioned that he was forced to do so under the threat of losing public funding. Does that say it all, or what? Who are they protecting, and from what are they protecting us?

We can change things. Sex is neither "good" nor "bad." It is a fundamental part of our lives. Physical attraction is often the catalyst that leads to lasting relationships. Our perception of sex depends on who we are and who we want to be. Our highest choice is to enjoy sex in the spirit of love of self and share that love with our partner. When we see our naked bodies as beautiful, we are able to appreciate that same beauty in art and in other people. We can then pass that appreciation on to our children, creating a positive cycle. Sex will no longer be something to hide, but rather a celebration of life. Sex is a beautiful part of life, setting us free, rejuvenating us, enabling us with the mysterious power to bring new life into the world, and providing an opportunity to experience physical and spiritual joy.

CHAPTER 20

Relationships: Divorce

Do you remember the old line: "I didn't realize you were married. You look so happy." Whether we're formally married or just informally attached, separating can be one of the more traumatic events in our lives.

As human beings, we need varying degrees of sociality. That sociality inevitably builds relationships—the greater the intensity of the relationship, the greater the possibility of painful detachment. So, what can we do to smooth the separation process?

As any good Buddhist knows, attachment comes with risk. One solution is to refrain from attaching to anything or anyone. That way, we hedge against the impermanence of this world, never suffering loss when things change. Unfortunately, unless you enjoy living as a hermit, non-attachment is an unattractive option. A more reasonable approach is to enter into relationships in a way that allows us to recognize their impermanence and accept any separation as part of life's experience. In that way, any separation is neither good nor bad, but *just is*. Allowing a relationship to evolve without judgment or expectation provides greater freedom in which to understand and share each other's experiences. We increase the chances of success by removing our egos from the equation. In the event that the relationship dissolves, it becomes less "personal" and more a natural transition in emotional and spiritual growth.

The need for control determines why some separations turn into plate-throwing affairs and others are amiable.

Soothing our damaged egos at the expense of our partner is never productive. It has been said that love and hate are horns on the same bull. Familiarity brings with it the unique power to know exactly which buttons to press to annoy or hurt the other person.

I was witness to the nasty divorce of good friends where they argued over every stick of furniture and every fork and knife. They had managed to hurt each other's feelings to such an extent that they were desperately trying to repair the damage by reasserting themselves. Of course, that approach is less than effective, intensifying and prolonging the pain. It's called biting off your nose to spite your face, an unpleasant lesson in futility.

By contrast, I had two friends who separated peacefully, and are still working together in the family business. They never let their egos get in the way. They saw the big picture and accepted dissolution as an opportunity to grow rather than a personal failing. They maintained a certain respect for each other despite their differences. And, most of all, they preserved their inner peace never forgetting their spiritual connection. This is not just a pie-in-the-sky example. It can be done. How we perceive our spirituality greatly affects our attitude toward others. Recognizing a universal connection tempers our egos and helps us to see things from the other person's point of view. It reminds us that we are not the center of the universe.

An uncooperative partner can make things difficult. The road to resolution gets longer when a party refuses to be objective. Our drive for survival kicks in and sends a message to fight. We certainly don't want to become a victim. By allowing ourselves to be victimized, we lose our empowerment to change things. But we can protect ourselves and still respond to stubborn adversity in a constructive way.

It is possible to protect the property and people in our charge without ego interference. Objectivity is everything. It can be useful to involve an impartial third party where feelings run high. That person can be a catalyst in restoring perspective and priorities. That person can also be instrumental in saving the relationship. Most states have legislated for common property and scheduled child support. So, in difficult situations, guidelines are already in place, reducing potential areas of dispute. A positive attitude by one party can often cause the other party to realize his or her small-mindedness and become more reasonable.

The bottom line is that we do this to ourselves. The solution is within our control. We do not have to hurt each other. Separated or divorced parents, because of the continuing social requirements of their children, are going to be forced to interact for the rest of their lives—hopefully as friends. We enhance our physical and spiritual lives by making these responsibilities as pleasant as possible.

In a Divine Universe, we are all connected by the same spiritual energy. The other person doesn't have to be the enemy just because a relationship has ended. That person is an extension of us. How we treat that person reflects on how we wish to be treated. By recognizing our connection, the false needs of our egos, and the complexity of events, we empower ourselves to accept the breakup without hostility. We maintain compassion for the other person. And, most importantly, *we move on.* There is no greater loss than to waste the present moment mired in the past. The sooner we transition through dissolution of a relationship, the sooner we return to our life's work and personal fulfillment.

CHAPTER 21

Life's Work: On the Road

Midmorning finds me driving home from the bakery with a loaf of bread and the world's best cinnamon rolls. Rush-hour traffic has thinned and things are settling down. I signal for a right turn off the boulevard when a pickup truck zooms around me, cutting me off, the driver flipping me the bird. Apparently, he wants to let me know I wasn't going fast enough. My first reaction is one of anger. He has trampled my ego. I return the favor and flip him off before making my turn. Then, I catch myself. *What am I doing? Why am I playing his game? Is this who I want to be?*

Well, as dame fate would have it, after working my way through several side streets, I come out on another main street and pull up to a red light. Guess who is sitting next to me: the same pickup truck. We immediately see each other. With our windows down on this fine summer day, I feel compelled to smooth over our confrontation. More than a little embarrassed, I say, "Sorry for overreacting. I was just slowing down to make my turn." Just as embarrassed, he says, "I guess I was a little impatient. My boss has been on my ass all day. You just happened to be there."

And, just like that, there was positive resolution. It could as well have ended with two people, angry and upset, taking their frustration out on the next person they meet—you know, the negative multiplier effect.

Why is it that many of us change from Dr. Jekyll to Mr. Hyde when we step into our cars? Why is it that people who would never cut in line at the theater find it unnecessary to wait their turn on the highway? What is it about being in a car that obscures everyday social courtesy? Where does courtesy go when we get behind the wheel?

Is it because being in a vehicle provides us with anonymity? Without the scrutiny of identification, we are free to act in an antisocial manner. And that anonymity allows us to be less accountable. I probably wouldn't have acted as I did if I had known the other driver.

I almost lost it, but was able to redeem things. Upon quick reflection, I saw the folly of being mean-spirited toward another human being. My spiritual connection to him took control. He no longer posed a threat because I recognized my ego as the problem. That, in turn, empowered me to change the situation into a positive experience. Instead of road rage, we were able to see each other in an understanding way. And, just for a moment, I was reminded of the stress associated with travel.

We live in a mobile world. Travel time is a serious vocational consideration in terms of quality of life, both physical and spiritual. I have a friend who travels one hour to work, and one hour home. That's 12.5 percent of his sixteen waking hours. He is not alone. There are many like him, working a job in the city and living in the distant suburbs. With eight-plus hours at work and two hours on the road, he spends over 60 percent of his waking time away from home. Add a trip to the office on Saturdays, and he spends *most of his time* supporting a lifestyle for which he *doesn't have time*. Is that ironic or what? Perhaps a lesser-paying job closer to home, or a smaller house closer to the same job, would allow him to spend more time with his family. The quality of his life, including inner peace, is directly affected by his travel choices. Idyllic suburban life often costs more than money. Relative location is an important vocational decision. Let's look at some other important considerations.

CHAPTER 22
Life's Work: Vocation

The word, vocation, implies a calling. It suggests that our life's work be more than just something to do. It advocates work that provides fulfillment—allowing us to explore and develop who we are. Vocation includes many things, from full-time mother to corporate CEO, nuclear scientist to landscaper, butcher to professor, politician to ditch digger. Each person has a peculiar inclination toward his/her purpose. The trick is to recognize, embrace, and explore our calling.

I think back to a memorable line by Charles Bukowski, a popular underground writer of the 1960s, at one of his campus appearances. After a reading, he was seated at a table with several students. One student mentioned she might become a writer. In response to this rather uncommitted declaration of vocation, he replied, "You don't choose writing. Writing chooses you!" The line always stuck with me because it contains a pearl of wisdom: We must let our spiritual energy guide the choices in our lives. Decisions should not be formed by intellect alone. Our inner sense, or "gut feeling," will show us what we need. To receive that message, we must have a present consciousness or awareness. Following our intuition is the best way to find an appropriate vocation.

Developing present consciousness assists us in recognizing spiritual signs along the way. Our spirit will direct us to a fitting vocation, but we have to be conscious of the present if we are to recognize the signs. For example: when applying for a position, we realize that we have driven to the wrong address and missed the appointment. Is our error just a simple mistake, or is it a guiding sign? We need an active present awareness to recognize a suggestion such as this, and realize that perhaps the interview was not in our best vocational interest. Being in the right slot allows us to reach our potential and experience a useful, satisfying life. It is personally destructive to spend our whole life doing something we don't like.

There are helpful tools for finding and changing vocations. Prayer or meditation allows us to connect with our spirit and develop a consciousness. Some people use positive visualization to project an image of their ideal vocation. It is a meditative process whereby we visualize ourselves being exactly what we want to be. For instance, if we desire to be in the greenhouse business, we meditate and visualize ourselves in great detail as successful greenhouse operators, tending to our greenhouse plants, scheduling deliveries, and talking with customers. Athletes use positive visualization by thinking of themselves beating the clock, winning a medal, or enjoying public recognition. Positive imaging sends out powerful energy that has a strange way of causing the visualization to actually happen. It is commonly referred to as the "power of positive thinking." When a previsualized event actually occurs it is, in effect, our spirit providing us with what we need so that we can be who we want to be. Conversely, if we think negatively and send out negative energy, it creates and reinforces negative consequences. One grouch in the office can destroy a whole company's morale.

We should choose our life's work based on what truly satisfies us rather than on such things as status, power, or money. It is dependably true that we will succeed if we enjoy what we do. Better to work for a little less money and a little more satisfaction, especially when we spend the better part of our lives doing it. Which brings to mind a friend of mine. He has pretty much everything he could want. But, he has accumulated a fortune doing something he really doesn't like. He has all of the adult toys, but feels very unfulfilled. His life is caught up in a vicious cycle: working long hours—to provide for an extravagant lifestyle—that he doesn't have time to enjoy—because he's always working. Now, in his later years, he sees his wasted life with regret. He just doesn't know how to get off the hamster wheel.

A long time ago, he chose to pursue wealth regardless of personal cost. Being extremely competitive, and being enamored with our consumer culture, he lost sight of what's important. It's easy to do. Our competitive system emphasizes success mostly in monetary terms. We must step back and ask ourselves what we need, as opposed to what we want, and how much of ourselves we're willing to devote to those ends.

When we buy a new car, are we willing to work an extra day per year just to have seat warmers? When we select that car, are we willing to work an extra week per year just for the status of a special model or brand name? In a larger sense, if we consistently choose an embellished lifestyle, are we willing to compromise our vocational choices and perhaps work a job we don't like just to support spiritually empty aspirations? Life is full of trade-offs. Our choices regarding what's important—and what isn't—define who we are and who we want to be.

Some of us have limited opportunity because of conditions like mental or physical disabilities, lack of training, or economic constraints. Yet, we all know of people with severe limitations who play their difficult cards as if those cards were a winning hand. A positive attitude and realistic goals can provide us with the quiet, peaceful energy necessary for a satisfying life, despite adversity.

I sat next to a rather slow kid during my high school years. I knew he didn't get things as quickly as the rest of us, but he conscientiously pursued his studies. His books were dog-eared from use, the margins filled with notes. Our books looked like they were brand new. We were coasting while he worked like there was no tomorrow. As we approached the end of junior year, he began to catch up. I remember my instructors chiding me for not working as hard as him. He ended up graduating in the top third of our class and went on to a successful career. Every time I think of him, I remind myself to work to my ability.

It is possible to find peace in the right job if we maintain an awareness of what's important in life. Let's look at society's view of labor, the true contribution of work, and how compensation is determined.

CHAPTER 23
Life's Work: Dignity of Labor

Labor is generally thought of as physical work, though that's not necessarily the case. We can labor mentally as well. I speak of labor in its broadest vocational sense: physical or mental exertion to reach an objective.

We all share in the same Divinity. As a result, that shared spirituality becomes a part of everything we do, including our work. Whether we sweep floors or teach rocket science, there is equivalent dignity in every vocation. No job is less noble than another. Though abilities will vary by kind and degree, each person's output is worthy of respect.

Unfortunately, not every vocation is created equal. It is common in our marketplace culture to afford more dignity and respect to vocations that are highly paid. If there is a demand for your skills, your vocation will attract higher wages having little relationship to the job's societal contribution. That is why professional football players make millions while social workers make much less. The real mistake is to afford less dignity to the social worker's lower paying job. There is no relationship between pay and dignity. Pay is related to economic demand and, to a lesser degree, performance. Dignity is related to Divinity.

This all raises an interesting question: if everyone works to the highest level of his/her ability, shouldn't he or she share equally in the total benefit he or she has helped create? In an ideal world, the answer would be yes because the best we can do is work as hard and as efficiently as our talents will allow.

Yet, we all know reality is quite different. Our economic system gives greater reward to those who create a larger part of the pie regardless of how hard they work. Thus, someone born with an abundance of talent, in a job where there's a demand for that talent, can, without much effort, enjoy a disproportionately large part of the total pie. Conversely, someone born with little talent, in a low-demand job, but exerting maximum effort, may receive a disproportionately small piece of the total pie. Is that fair? An ideal social/economic system would provide reward based on effort and contribution to the common good. Ours could use some improvement. The important thing to remember is that dignity is inherent in honest effort regardless of economic consequence.

CHAPTER 24

Life's Work: Expectation

Vocational expectations have a profound influence on the way we live our lives. Reasonable goals provide a method for measuring our progress. Unreasonable goals create ongoing anxiety and disappointment when we inevitably fail.

I knew a self-made man who developed a machine-tool business. He was a farm boy from southern Ohio who started life with very little. Hard work coupled with an uncanny sense of people, led to economic success. Unfortunately, the control that helped him succeed became his downfall. He micromanaged every aspect of the operation. His days were torturous and long. His expectations were unrealistically high. He couldn't take a vacation for fear that one of his assistants would be unable to tend to things. In short, he was an extreme example of someone who believed he could control everything by the choices he made. His philosophy contained no room for chance. Control was everything. His anxiety eventually caused physical problems that killed him. He passed away young and wealthy. Oops! Game over. "Do not pass "Go." Do not collect $200." But outsiders saw it differently—his success was directly related to some timely breaks that made all the difference, breaks beyond his control.

I met a restaurant owner in Rockland, Maine, who was willing to talk about his success. He had managed a popular local eatery for more than fifteen years—no small feat in a one-year-and-gone-type business. Most nights, you couldn't get a table without a reservation. He enjoyed sitting with his customers, talking with them as if they were family. He attributed his success to "passion, hard work, a tolerable degree of ignorance, and a generous amount of luck." He said this jokingly but really meant it. By so doing, he readily acknowledged an appreciation for events beyond his control and their part in his success.

Our expectations should respect the complexity of life. The best of choices sometimes fail. Our control is limited. Accepting what comes along is important. The notion of outside influence can be a friend or an enemy. Acceptance reduces the anxiety of unrealistic expectation and the disappointment of failure. And in a backhanded way, *allows* success to occur.

CHAPTER 25
Life's Work: Success

It is easy to mistake wealth for success. Success can take the form of many things—such as money, recognition, power, fame, and achievement. But it can also be something far more beneficial—an opportunity for spiritual growth. For example, success can enable us to financially assist in feeding the hungry or fighting AIDS, cancer, or other diseases. It can allow us to use our fame as a springboard for causes like environmental initiatives. True success, in the context of a Divine Universe, helps us to make the highest spiritual choices and has a positive effect on all things.

The accumulation of wealth brings with it spiritual issues. The question is how much "stuff" do we really need? A common progression for people approaching enlightenment and Mastery is to give up most of their worldly possessions. They give them up, neither because the possessions are inherently "bad," nor because the possessions obstruct the path to enlightenment. Rather, they relinquish them because they have no need for nonessential things of the world. One of the highest spiritual choices a wealthy person can make is to use that wealth for the benefit of others. In choosing to share, we acknowledge that we are an interrelated part of the Divine Universe, and that a complex web of events played a part in our good fortune. By virtue of our mortality, we are merely tenants of this world and therefore, can truly *own* nothing. At best, we are only capable of temporary possession. We have a duty to use only what we need and to manage the excess for the benefit of everyone. Which returns us full circle to the question, how much is enough? The answer is subjective. It depends on our level of spirituality. Generally, the greater our spiritual development, the less we need, and the less we worry about such things. One of the pitfalls of getting lost in success can be identity crisis.

Have you ever met people who ask how you are doing, and then go on to use your answer as a springboard for a dissertation on their success? They need recognition to support their identity. It is a common ego trap. These people are defining who they are by their accomplishments. Unfortunately, they are headed for inevitable disappointment. Present success rarely continues indefinitely. It is unrealistic to expect that things will remain the same. The inevitable changes of tomorrow jeopardize a success-based identity. Who we are should be defined by our good judgment rather than the judgment of others. When we live for the approval of others, they own us. It is better to develop our identity on a personal/spiritual basis. A successful vocation enhances our spiritual life by giving us purpose and fulfillment, providing a stable foundation for the development of our character. In that context, we should regularly reassess who we are and who we want to be. Who we are is also directly related to our physical existence. Good health is necessary if our body is to carry out our intentions successfully.

CHAPTER 26
Health: Eating Habits and Food Choices

My stomach tells me it's past noon and my stomach is never wrong! Time to refuel. I respect the needs of my humble, familiar shell because it is the instrumentality that allows me to *experience Being*. It is a physical temple that houses my Essence, my Divinity. It requires thoughtful nourishment. Proper eating can be spiritual as well as physical, requiring some monitoring and reflection.

How and why we eat has a profound impact on how much we eat. Unfortunately, we eat too much. Obesity is fast becoming America's leading health concern. It contributes directly, or indirectly, to most health problems such as diabetes and heart disease.

Before we blame ourselves for simply failing to close our mouths, compassion is in order. History plays a part in the genes we inherit. Scientists now know that the satiation gene is turned off in some people, forcing them to experience persistent hunger. It is also known that some people are born with an unhealthy taste for sugar, fat, and salt. Others acquire unhealthy habits from their culture, habits that become very difficult to break. Still, others are born with an anxious personality, conducive to overeating. Some are born with a propensity for addiction to many things, including food. And many of us eat poorly because of deceptive advertising and product information. *Sheesh*, how can anyone be skinny?

"Big Food" is clearly guilty of encouraging obesity. Food advertising is deceptive regarding recommended serving sizes; no one has just "one cup" of cereal in the morning. So, the 200 calories per "serving" information is based on an unrealistic premise. They don't want you to know that you are, in fact, consuming about 400 calories using a normal size bowl, adding some milk. Big Food allocates disproportionately large sums of money for advertising sugar-filled foods to the under-twelve-year-old group; catch Saturday morning cartoons to see how clever this advertising has become. Big Food knows that childhood eating habits carry forward into adulthood and are resistant to change. They continue to present cereal foods as healthy just because they contain fiber, ignoring their caloric impact. And they continue to promote snack foods with unhealthy amounts of sugar, salt, and saturated fat because these processed foods increase their bottom line (as well as adding heavily to our "bottom line"!). But wait, we haven't even touched on the meat industry with its "well-marbled" steaks and "juicy" chops (code for laced with saturated fat). And don't forget those darlings of obesity, the fast-food industry.

I recently ate at a fast-food place because my grandkids insisted. Being a fast-food newbie, I ordered an apparently "harmless" apple-pie dessert. When I checked the ingredients/calories, I was shocked to find that one small roll (about six bites) contained thirteen grams of saturated fat and about 300 calories. The little bugger was an open-heart special. Add a cheeseburger, fries, soft drink, and you have, in one meal, most of your daily recommended calories, plus enough saturated fat for two days! Is this really who we want to be? Or, is there a reasonable alternative?

Perhaps a change of perspective is in order. What if we step back and take a breath? Eating is spiritual as well as physical. It provides an opportunity to experience a most intimate

Divinity connection—awareness of our place in the food chain. It can be used as a moment to reflect and meditate.

Allowing time for food awareness is spiritually and physically advantageous. Rushing through our meal, with the TV blaring, encourages overeating and digestive problems. We should consciously relate to our food in every way. In a slower, focused environment, we see, smell, and taste food with intensity. We allow ourselves to feel its texture and hear it crunch. By so doing, we elevate this simple task to a physical/spiritual celebration, one bite at a time. Slowing the process also allows us to be mindful of portions and satisfaction levels. By eating this way, we develop and enhance an awareness of our connection to our food and the larger world as we strengthen our present consciousness.

It's been said that we are what we eat. In a Divine Universe, where everything is spiritually connected, our food choices take on new meaning. No longer does that baked ham come from "just a pig." Instead it comes from a creature that has a spiritual nature like us. We, the dominant species, are responsible for ultimate decisions of what shall live, and what shall be consumed. Needless killing shows a disregard for the spirituality of the victims. We don't consume food without consequences. Our choices affect everything around us. Those choices should promote the greatest good and the least damage while eliminating as much waste as possible. It is our responsibility, at the top of the food chain, to sensitively manage all subservient food resources.

I visited a state-of-the-art egg farm some years ago and was repulsed by what I saw. There were thousands of chickens, two to a wire cage, in long raised rows in a windowless building with lights on twenty-four hours a day. The chickens hardly had room to move. They couldn't even turn around. A front conveyor trough brought in food. A rear conveyor trough removed waste. Eggs rolled into collection baskets below. Each chicken lasted about six months in this environment and was then slaughtered. Because of overcrowding, unusually large amounts of antibiotics were needed to overcome immune system breakdowns and rampant disease. Management had become hardened, rationalizing the cruelty as a trade-off for productivity and low prices, demanded by uncaring wholesalers, retailers, and consumers.

Most of us have become disconnected from our food sources. We have never seen a commercial chicken/egg farm. Urban living and specialization of labor have evolved to a point where most of us don't *feel* the effects of our food choices. It's easy to eat chicken when we haven't had to personally kill, drain, pluck, and butcher them. It's easy to eat veal when we haven't seen the restriction pens where young bulls have no room to move, promoting muscle atrophy, and consequently more-tender meat. You don't want to be born a boy cow! In short, the ostrich approach effectively shields us from reality.

Perhaps we should all look into the cloudy eyes of cattle crowded into a cattle truck, bound for market, as they wallow in their own vomit and fecal matter. That might make a difference in what we decide to order for dinner. We are responsible for those animals, as if we had raised them ourselves. We must ask if we have the right to abuse them and take their lives when quality food substitutes are available.

Old MacDonald's farm is a myth. Such an idyllic pastoral image of farming has no relationship to reality. Our food is not produced that way. Today, large, specialized farms produce vegetables, grains, and food animals. Quantity is everything. The cost pressure of huge processors and retailers has caused farmers to use nonsustainable and inhumane practices just to stay in business. The only way they can survive is to spread their overhead across a larger number of food units. Generally speaking, a quantity-driven food system leads to a quality-deprived food system. Production pressure leads to overcrowding and disease. In the process, today's farms produce food in a shortsighted way, depleting water and soil, while polluting the air.

For example, we continue to draw down, for agricultural irrigation, the immense Ogallala Aquifer, an underground water source beneath eight adjoining western states. I recently spoke with friends who had visited their extended family in West Texas. Their relatives are engaged in large-scale farming, using underground water from the aquifer. The family said that ten years ago they had to drill only 300 feet to reach water. Today, they must drill 700 feet. The aquifer is disappearing in spite of its incredible size. And yet, farmers in these states have no comprehensive long-term plan for aquifer sustainability. They just keep drilling deeper, depleting this resource as if it were limitless. It should be noted that, without irrigation, this region couldn't sustain a small pumpkin patch, let alone large-scale commercial agriculture.

Long-term costs of nonsustainable farming, such as depletion of the Ogallala Aquifer, are not included in present retail pricing. We pass the buck to future generations. Unfortunately, this cost-driven system is the antithesis of a sustainable, quality-oriented, humane food connection. It has brought low-cost food of dubious quality to those in the cities and stressed living conditions for those who produce the food. In a Divine Universe it is our responsibility to look at more than just price. We must examine the true cost of the people and resources involved.

By being selective shoppers, we can make a difference. Some food stores provide point-of-purchase information on food source, quality standards, sustainability practices, and man-made chemical usage. They also describe how livestock, fowl, and fish were raised. Many coffee shops sell only "free trade" coffee and beans, thereby representing that the producer has been paid a living wage. Organic foods now account for about 4 percent of total U.S. grocery volume and are rapidly increasing their share of the total food market.

At first blush, these products appear to cost more. However, their prices merely reflect the *actual* cost of sustainable, humane, agricultural practices. Getting reconnected with our food system empowers us to force physical and spiritual change through intelligent consumer choices. An organic apple a day keeps the doctor—and pesticides—away!

CHAPTER 27
Health: Environment/Lifestyle

Environment and lifestyle have a major influence on our health. Unfortunately, we still don't get the message. We continue to pollute our world. Our lifestyles reveal a narcissistic and self-indulgent culture. We fail to appreciate our spiritual connection with everything around us.

This failure is evidenced in many ways by the choices we make. We drive large fuel-inefficient vehicles, not for need of space, but because they are stylish, thereby wasting resources and adding to global pollution. We join the Sierra Club but think nothing of applying chemical weed killers, pesticides, and fertilizers on our lawns just for aesthetics. In our homes we use "throwaway" paper and plastic products when long-lasting substitutes are available. We consume processed foods with carcinogens, saturated fats, and hydrogenated oils. Choices such as these adversely affect our health and well-being.

On a global scale, poor ecological practices produce tainted water, polluted air, depleted soil, toxic chemicals in the food chain, and concern that long-term thermal affects will change our climate and threaten life, as we know it. Ozone warning days are now mostly ignored, even though the danger is so serious that we are advised to limit outdoor activity and take special care if we are elderly or have respiratory problems. Most untreated surface water is unfit to drink due to the presence of human waste and chemical toxins. Many of these toxins are related to cancers and nervous disorders.

The question is, do we *want* to change things? The first step is to take personal responsibility for the consequences of our acts. When we blame others or wait for others to change things, we give up our power. Only by accepting responsibility can we empower ourselves and make a difference—think globally, act locally.

I often run through a beautiful city park and see the same elderly woman carrying a plastic bag. She strolls the paths, collecting waste cans, bottles, and trash. It appears to be her personal environmental contribution. She is changing things, one candy wrapper at a time. Her example is small but powerful.

From an ecological point of view, "What goes around comes around." Our good health depends on how we treat our environment—and ourselves. We should make only the highest choices that are in our best interest and the best interests of all other people and things.

CHAPTER 28
Health: Medical Care

Much has been written (and churches have been organized) regarding the concept of self-healing and the influence of mind and spirit over body. People in test groups, given a disguised sugar pill rather than the actual pharmaceutical pill, often respond positively. We know from these tests that the mind can influence the body and affect its health for better or worse. Quantum physics has demonstrated that we have the power to influence our physical world by the way we project energy. And yet, we focus on biological treatment with little, if any, attention to the mental or spiritual aspects. Anyone who has been in a hospital knows how doctors fail to make a serious effort to understand a patient's psychology or theology, and how those factors might be causing or exacerbating a biological problem. Doctors' reluctance to spend time listening is a major failing of Western medicine. Fortunately, there is much that we can do on a spiritual level to maintain and enhance our health.

Through prayer and meditation we can use positive visualization to enhance an image of ourselves as a healthy person. This projection of positive energy allows our spirit to bring us what we need to fulfill the image. Our mind becomes comfortable with the idea of good health, and begins to think about the subject in a beneficial way. It directs the body to take whatever measures are necessary to experience good health. In our present consciousness we begin to make choices that encourage good health.

For example, we may have developed a long-term weight problem that has adversely affected our overall mental and physical health. As a consequence, our self-esteem has suffered, creating a self-defeating cycle of depression and overeating. We begin our rehabilitation by praying or meditating to connect with our spiritual side. We visualize ourselves as attractive, healthy people at normal weight. As we repeat this practice, our spirit enables the mind to embrace that image. The mind motivates the body to do the things necessary to lose weight, including getting psychological help, if necessary. The body responds by exercising and eating right. The mind then reinforces the process by noticing the improvement and bolstering our self-image. And throughout the rehabilitation we use our present consciousness to make advantageous choices that facilitate the improvement. Thinking healthy is the first step toward being healthy.

There are times, however, when we aren't capable of healing ourselves. On those occasions, outside help may be needed. Surgical procedure or medication may be necessary. It is especially important, when relinquishing medical control to another, to touch base with our spiritual side. Recognizing that our spiritual nature is not subject to medical success or failure removes fear from the equation. Knowing that our spirit will prevail, with or without the body, can be a source of great comfort, making any outcome easier to accept.

When it comes to medication, we have pills for just about everything. Prescription drugs are a part of our lifestyle. Even incidental pain is no longer accepted as a part of life's experience. Pharmaceutical companies cleverly present consumer advertising so that suggested illness symptoms apply to healthy individuals as well (code for creating a demand where none exists). Consumers respond by pressuring their physicians to provide medication that may not be necessary. "I want the purple pill," even if I'm not sure it will help me. In short, we expect a miracle pill for every discomfort, and the pharmaceutical industry is happy to encourage and accommodate us. By so doing, we ignore our internal healing powers, encouraging a dependency on outside help.

The culprit is pain and how we deal with it. The world can be a painful place. Our culture refuses to accept everyday pain as a part of life. It is certainly in our best interest to minimize pain, but it is also healthy to realize that experiencing pain is inevitable. It is as valid an experience as joy and should be understood that way. So, how do we deal with this difficult aspect of life? It's helpful to step outside our body to remind ourselves that pain affects only the body. The spirit cannot be diminished by pain. No matter how badly the body suffers, the spirit remains untouched. Through meditation or prayer, we can learn to withdraw from the body into a "safe" place where pain cannot hurt us. This practice of passive acceptance is the cornerstone of inner peace. Over the long haul, it is much more valuable than a pill for every ill, especially as our bodies undergo aging with increased health issues.

CHAPTER 29
Health: Aging

In our narcissistic culture, where we idolize youth, aging doesn't fit well. We are determined to ignore our eventual physical and mental decline. As a result, we postpone the inevitable until it can no longer be avoided. In the process, we squander an opportunity to appreciate our physical evolution and understand the connection to our spiritual journey.

I knew a woman who was truly beautiful in her youth. She attracted attention wherever she went. She built her life around her good looks. When those looks began to fade, she became obsessed with hiding her physical decline. She started wearing excessive makeup to hide wrinkles; undersized shoes to hide enlarged feet; wigs to hide baldness; unusually strong perfume; and clothes that were a size too small. She avoided being included in photographs so as not to have her decline recorded. Gradually, as her age advanced, she avoided going out in public for fear of being seen. Eventually, she became a prisoner of her vanity, isolated and bitter.

Our failure to age gracefully betrays a lack of spiritual understanding. The body is just a shell, necessary for experiencing life. It is finite and mortal. As it ages, it wears out. That is a natural consequence. On the other hand, our spirit never wears out. It existed before the body and will exist after the body. It cannot be harmed by the physical demise of the body. Wouldn't we be better advised to focus on the spirit? Nothing physical really matters. We hear people say things like "beauty is only skin deep," and "it's the heart that counts."

Isn't that an effort to acknowledge the folly of emphasizing physical attributes over spiritual substance? I suggest that people with inner peace and contentment find it much easier to laugh at aging, knowing the foolhardiness of worshiping the body. Their journey is spiritual, not physical. They see the pain and limitations of aging as just another part of life, neither good nor bad, just something to be experienced. And, it seems that they have a certain inner beauty that comes forth on a physical level, even as their body deteriorates. Sometimes a positive attitude about our personal health isn't enough. We must also protect ourselves from outside hazards.

CHAPTER 30
Health: Hazards

In the late eighteen hundreds, Joshua Slocum, the first man to sail alone around the world, overcame many natural obstacles but almost failed because of human aggression. For three years he struggled with ocean storms, equipment failure, and extreme isolation, hardships one would expect on an epic sea journey. But the greatest test came as he attempted to sail around the tip of South America, near Cape Horn, westbound for the Pacific. That area lacked any rule of law. Sailing through the Strait of Magellan, he was repeatedly attacked by local tribes especially at night when he anchored and slept. Knowing that the attackers didn't wear shoes, he spread tacks on the deck of his boat each night. When barefooted pirates attempted to quietly board the boat, they would inadvertently step on the tacks, sounding a painful warning. Because of his cunning, he was able to successfully ward off his attackers and continue on. But for his resourcefulness and weapons, he would have been a dead man.

Examining this story from a spiritual point of view, we must ask: in a Divine Universe, would Slocum have had a right to take the lives of his assailants? We all have a natural right to life, but that right becomes complicated when we are forced to compete with another life. We should take life only to ensure our survival. It is a logical extension to defend against deadly aggression, including preemptive action if the aggression is imminent. With the shoe on the other foot, when we accidentally step on a hornet's nest and get stung, we must remember that we are experiencing the consequences of a right to life, further down the food chain.

Some people may accuse me of taking too much liberty in allowing even "justified" killing. They hold that violence is never justified. Pacifists believe that violence only begets more violence. The great Mahatma Gandhi, by setting an example of peaceful resistance, saved India from civil war and the loss of hundreds of thousands of lives. Buddhist monks avoid killing any kind of life including insects and spiders. There is much to be gleaned from this philosophy. The question is, whether nonviolence will assure survival of the species in a world of terrorists and religious fanatics.

Society must constrain people who exhibit dangerous antisocial behavior. Some states execute criminals for extreme violation of the law. But is execution necessary when incarceration provides a suitable alternative for removal? There is no evidence that governments enforcing the death penalty have any better crime deterrence than those without it. Can we justify taking life in this way? Is vengeance ever acceptable? Can we evolve to a higher level while disregarding our Divinity?

On the other hand, can we allow fringe lunatics to destroy our world? It is getting increasingly difficult to identify the enemy. Armies no longer line up and face each other. The "bad guys" don't wear black hats anymore. Exploding a "dirty" bomb in an urban area will cause more harm than any army could. How should we treat these dangerous people? In a Divine Universe we must balance survival with a humane approach to those who would do us harm. Many radicals are a product of past violence. Until we break the cycle, additional violence will only produce more radicals. Understanding their history is critical to any meaningful progress. Consideration, kindness, and tolerance should be our guidelines.

CHAPTER 31
Spirituality: Meditation

I set aside my writing, and walk out into the backyard. It's about 4:00 p.m. This is my quiet time. I place a folding chair under an old sugar maple and plop down on it, conforming to its shape. The day has been challenging. I've managed to lose my inner peace on more than one occasion—a betrayal of my ability to consistently sort out the important from the trivial. This is my opportunity to refocus on the present moment. Crimson leaves float down like feathers. As I feel them drift onto my head and shoulders, I am reminded of my great connection to all things. And, slowly, sliding into meditation, the burden of everyday life melts away refreshing my perspective.

We need some quiet time each day to renew our spiritual connection through prayer or meditation. Though they are similar, I prefer meditation because it tends to focus on our participation *in* the Divinity of the universe rather than appealing *to* a Divine entity *outside* the universe. Meditation is a celebration of our connection rather than our separation from all else. It can be used in conjunction with any religion or no religion. We need no special place of worship and it can be used at any time of day. The hard part is remembering to do it, especially when life gets busy. Luckily, the easy part is its simplicity—like breathing in and breathing out.

One of the best books on meditation is *The Joy of Living* by Yongey Mingyur. He explains meditation in a way that makes it available to everyone at any spiritual level. This is no monk in an ivory tower. His good humor and grasp of reality distinguish him as a special teacher and compassionate human being. He emphasizes frequency over duration as the key to a rewarding practice. You don't have to visit a mountaintop guru or be a hermit to enjoy the benefits. He shows how to enrich everyday life without joining a monastery. Regular meditation is the foundation for developing awareness or consciousness. We must appreciate and live in the present moment if we are to experience the full extent of *Being*.

CHAPTER 32
Spirituality: Mysticism

Present awareness enables us to connect with the power of the universe and its mystical aspects. I once asked a Protestant pastor how he would enjoy his leisure time if he weren't so busy with his ministry. He responded unequivocally and without hesitation that he would pray constantly. The inference was clear: he loved the "high" of being connected and needed nothing more. Mysticism is all about experiencing that strange connection. I would define mysticism as experiencing reality beyond perceptual and intellectual reason—in short, consciousness of connection to a higher spiritual plane.

We've all heard of people who have experienced an unexpected life-changing spiritual event. They often attribute these mystical experiences to their religious beliefs. But, are mystical happenings necessarily confined to one set of beliefs? We have evidence to the contrary. People of many institutionally religious beliefs, as well as agnostics and atheists, have all experienced these phenomena. So, they must all have something in common, other than their religious preferences. I suggest it's an awareness that allows them to tap into the energy of the Divine Universe, an experience available to all of us.

Many ordinary people, without unusual knowledge or tendency toward superstition, and without any special gifts or powers have had mystical experiences. Some last longer, and are stronger than others. There doesn't seem to be any rhyme or reason as to how or why they occur.

Some skeptics refer to mysticism as seeing what we wish to see. It is possible that we physically induce a state of euphoria and that there is nothing spiritual about it. Physiological manipulation of the brain by activities such as fasting, drugs, and/or isolation, can produce hallucinations similar to mystical experiences. But, that explanation appears rather inadequate according to those who have had the experience.

A close friend explained his experience this way: "A few years ago, I was driving down a busy city street, having a rather uneventful "same-old, same-old morning," when a profound calmness came over me. My surroundings suddenly felt much more intimate and real. Colors and sounds were more vivid. My awareness of this connection grew stronger and more understandable. There was a feeling of immense intelligence and creativity. I experienced a great peacefulness. There was a deep sense that the experience contained all of existence. I remember thinking that nothing could bother or harm me, and wondered how I might extend the experience. My sense of well-being and connection to all things was without boundaries. The experience lasted for several hours."

He said that if someone could grant him one wish, it would be to constantly live in such euphoria where *nothing else matters*. It is reasonable to believe that we all touch on mystical experiences from time to time, but don't always recognize them because they may be subtler or less noticeable. They aren't always life-changing epiphanies. Rather, they seem to occur in varying degrees of intensity, experienced by those who consciously, or unconsciously have the necessary level of awareness.

Mysticism is a powerful experience. It strongly suggests that there's more to this world than meets the eye. It creates an enlarged capacity for spiritual insight. We all have access to a higher spiritual plane. Isn't that intriguing? The important thing is to share the message with others. It is not enough to capture an enlightened state and stay in it, selfishly ignoring all else. Meditating in a state of euphoria in our cave is not productive. We have an opportunity to spread that sense of peace. Universal consciousness should be our goal.

CHAPTER 33
Last Light: One Candle

My body submits to fatigue as the day comes to an end. Through the window I see the glow of twilight that reminds me of a studio I once had on the fifth floor of an old warehouse. It had a magnificent westward view of the city skyline. In the foreground stood another old warehouse with a rooftop water tower. That tower was a roost for hundreds of pigeons. Each evening around dusk, the entire flock would suddenly take flight. They would fly as an ever-changing silver-gray dollop, lofting and diving, enlarging and contracting, sometimes dividing and then reuniting, never going far from the roost. Just as they approached the tower, the leader would draw them out for another loop, as if the fantasy deserved one last encore. Isn't it interesting that these simple birds found time each evening to collectively celebrate the dying light? Was their flight a defiance of darkness and the vulnerability it brings?

It's 9:00 p.m. as shadows absorb the light, filling the nooks and crannies of the house—shadows that still manage to fill the hearts of man with fear. So, I light a small candle. Perhaps we are that candle, pushing back the darkness, against all odds, as we plod through life trying to deal with the unknown, drawing strength from its glow.

CHAPTER 34
Last Light: Death

As sentient, highly evolved, biological entities, we are capable of awareness. That ability allows us to comprehend *Being*, including recognition of spirituality and mortality. Because we know we exist, we know we will die. Is it possible to laugh at our inevitable demise? Yes—if we understand that "life" is purely biological, as opposed to "existence" which is eternal—and the fact that we have nothing to fear.

We have evolved to be apprehensive about uncertainty, including, upon death, the loss of friends, family, and familiar places. Fear of the unknown has protected us since ancient times by causing us to be alert and wary. It is difficult to override a feeling so deep-seated and trustworthy. Nevertheless, we can approach death rationally. A good starting point is to ask how much of our fear is attributable to afterlife punishment, that is, a fear of God.

Our culture is heaven/hell oriented. The judgmental aspects of religious belief have colored our perspective of death. Under that influence, it's easy for the best of us to live and die in fear. But there is an enlightened alternative to fear.

In a Divine Universe, we are a part of God. There is no "judgment" day because there is no "good" or "evil." There is nothing to fear. We have fulfilled our biological purpose and move into further existence. We can die with a chuckle knowing that the riddle of life remains intact. And we should be able to die as we wish.

Our right to life comes with a right to die. And yet, in reality, that is not the case. We shoot horses when they break their leg. We mercy-kill adored family pets when they are beyond help. Even states that condone capital punishment go to great lengths to ensure that murderers are executed quickly by lethal injection. We do these things to reduce suffering. However, we won't allow suffering human beings to end life, even though they sign a document to that effect. Instead, we force them to wait for "natural" death after we disconnect their life support. We have the medical means and ability to assist suffering people by inducing immediate death (euthanasia). But that is prohibited because of laws against assisted suicide. These laws are a charade. They pretend to be a legal method of protecting people from being put to sleep against their will. In reality, they are the unconstitutional imposition of ancient religious doctrine holding suicide to be a sin. Whether we pull the plug and let people die, or assist them in dying by injecting toxins, we're interfering with the natural progression of things. Both constitute active intervention. Laws restraining one but not the other are logically inconsistent and ethically indefensible. Stringent safeguards are already in place for discontinuing life support. They require written consent of the patient and signatures from family and physicians. Those consent requirements could be the basis for rules on assisted death. It is unethical and unconscionable to force patients and families to go through a prolonged dying process. It delays closure, causes much pain and suffering, and results in drastically increased costs.

Suicide is a matter of natural right. We have a right to die as we wish. No civil law has standing to deny that right. Any such law is without authority and, even if it had authority, would be a blatant unconstitutional intrusion into one's spiritual beliefs.

After death, families are confronted with the unpleasant realities of such things as body disposal and funeral gatherings. Funerals are like small towns that cultural freeways bypassed long ago. They are badly in need of an update.

I recently attended a friend's funeral. It happened to be in the Roman Catholic tradition, but was fairly representative of most arrangements. I watched helplessly as the family grieved during a period of several days. They were trapped at a funeral home alongside the dead body in order to greet visitors. The corpse had been made up to look like a plastic version of the person I knew. Visitors took turns kneeling at the casket. Is it delusional to talk to a dead body? From time to time, group prayers were offered that referred to the deceased as a sinner, now awaiting judgment. They beseeched God's forgiveness. Expensive, perishable flower arrangements were everywhere—the family could have used that money for needed things. The eulogy was peppered with the need for God's mercy. The coffin was closed with expected emotional trauma. Thereafter, we drove on dangerous roads in a white-out snowstorm to the cemetery where we slipped and slid in dress shoes, carrying the casket up a steep, snow-covered hill to the gravesite. The family then experienced more suffering as the "dust to dust" invocation was delivered and mourners shoveled dirt on the casket. I stood there, frozen to the bone, in utter disbelief.

Why do we persist in honoring these painful, archaic customs? The dead body no longer harbors biological life, its remaining mass being converted into another energy form. The new form becomes deteriorating matter. Accept death as a biological conclusion but celebrate continuation of that person's Divine Energy. If we understand that concept, the body becomes available as an educational cadaver for teaching purposes, organ transplants, or research. And retirement by cremation becomes an ecologically acceptable option. I realize that some people have religious beliefs regarding resurrection of the body, and therefore want to keep the body complete and in one place. But they should take comfort in knowing that a God capable of such redemption would certainly be capable of reconstructing a body, whether merely decomposed or cremated.

There is need for a more comforted perspective of dying. Present customs and beliefs subject the dying and survivors to unnecessary suffering. Remove guilt and fear from the equation, and we have peace in our last moments. Accept death as a part of life, and it becomes easier to deal with the loss. Understand the process as continuous renewal, and enjoy the humor in our clumsy efforts to grasp the mystery.

CHAPTER 35

Last Light: Afterlife

$E = mc^2$. No energy is ever lost. So, Albert, what happens to our Energy when the body dies?

We exist as Divine Energy before we are born, while we are alive, and after we die. Birth and death are merely biological markers defining the parameters of a "life" experience.

After death, our Energy continues as a logical extension of our Divinity. Does that energy change to another form, or is it absorbed back into the larger energy of the universe? The possibilities are fascinating.

Regarding existence after death, some philosophers suggest the possibility of a continuing awareness of self, or self-consciousness. If this were true, all deceased beings would be aware beyond their biological death. And, if we think in terms of Perpetual Time, all beings, past, present, and future, would have awareness because of contemporaneous existence. That would mean there is an eternal presence and consciousness of all things at the present moment. The existence of such a presence is consistent with a timeless universe, the theory of Universal Energy, and Universal Unity. Would our comprehensive awareness allow us to communicate with all things of all time? Is that going on right now on a spiritual level? Is universal awareness reflected in our glimpses of the past and future in our present life? Without biological "life" and awareness as we know it, "eternal existence" becomes impossible to define. So, we can only speculate.

GERALD F. PENCA

The present moment is all that exists, with possible pre-life, life, and afterlife awareness being nothing more than a single, constant experience. The traditional timeline is an illusion.

CHAPTER 36
Last Light: Peace

I snuff out the candle and walk outside. The night sky dazzles with stars everywhere and an old moon rising. A soft, moist, southerly breeze rustles the willow leaves. Lying down on the damp cedar deck, I lose myself in a Divine Universe.

Wings

I close my tired eyes and drift away
To forest glade, a weathered mossy door
At end of deep wood path where spirits play
My quiet place, still beckons as before
A latchkey violates the sleeping lock
Allowing me to pass beyond the portal
Mist-thick white light reveals a handless clock
In timeless place where all things are immortal
My buoyant body drifts though seems connected
To meadows near and ancestors of old
A feeling of great joy and being protected
As future, past, and present lives unfold
   Humbled by death's mystical bequest
   And, peaceful now, *because I am*, at rest . . .

About the Author

Gerald Penca has experienced a varied life, as a professional musician, industrial engineer, attorney, and commercial/fine art photographer. Through it all, he has intermittently returned to his first love, writing prose and poetry. *Because I Am* is Gerald's first book. It pulls together a lifelong interest in the relationship between spirituality and the physical universe. Building on scientific fact, he logically develops an all-encompassing theory of a Divine Universe and our connection to all things. An entertaining day-in-the-life narrative illustrates how application of the theory can enrich our lives.

Printed in the USA
CPSIA information can be obtained
at www.ICGtesting.com
LVHW051146131023
760674LV00050B/771